Assessment of Learning

Our other publication by
Prof. S.K. Mangal and Prof. Shubhra Mangal

— Assessment of Learning
— Creating an Inclusive School
— Childhood and Growing up
— Learning and Teaching
— अधिगम का आकलन
— समेकित विद्यालय की स्थापना
— बाल्यकाल एवं वृद्धि-उन्मुख बालक
— अधिगम एवं शिक्षा

Assessment of Learning

Prof. S.K. Mangal
M.A., M.Sc., M.Ed., Ph.D. (Education)

Prof. (Mrs.) Shubhra Mangal
M.Sc., M.Ed., M.Phil, Ph.D. (Education)

SHIPRA

(First Published in India in 2017)

Rs. 750, US$ 25

ISBN: 978-93-86262-35-6

2023 Impression

Assessment of Learning

Published by:
SHIPRA PUBLICATIONS
LG 18-19, Pankaj Central Market,
I.P. Ext., Patparganj, Delhi 110092
+ 91 11 22235152/ 6152; 9650028065
info@shiprapublication.com
www.shiprapublication.com

Preface

What type of learning experience should be provided for a student in a teaching-learning context, the decision in this regard can only be well taken by making assessment and diagnosis of his or her potential, previous knowledge, abilities and capacities for such learning. The assessment of such nature is termed as "assessment for learning" and it needs to be carried out throughout the total process of teaching-learning from beginning till end. It is also named as formative or constructive assessment as it helps the construction and creation of knowledge on the part of students at their own quite independently or in collaboration or guidance from their teachers, peers and elders. Thus now a days in the changed perspective of the teaching-learning process guided by constructivist approach much emphasis is laid over 'assessment for learning' rather than the 'assessment of learning', a type of summative evaluation which has dominated the field of teaching-learning uptill now.

However, both types of evaluation—Formative and Summative governed by the terms 'Assessment for Learning' and 'Assessment of Learning' are very much needed for controlling the total process of teaching-learning to achieve the desired educational goals or objectives.

How such evaluation can be carried out and what type of tools and techniques (including those emerging from new trends) are available for carrying out these both types of assessment—'assessment for learning' and 'assessment of learning', it should be well known on the part of teachers serving in our schools. The best opportunity for equipping them with such knowledge is their teacher preparation course. It is why NCTE has issued directives to the universities and teacher education institution to bring modifications in their B.Ed. curriculum. Accordingly Guru Govind Singh Indraprastha University, New Delhi his introduced a compulsory paper named 'Assessment of Learning' in its two years B.Ed program.

The present text is specifically designed to meet the requirements of this paper. Although here it is specifically meant to cover the requirement of GGS Indraprastha University's prescribed syllabus, yet on account of its wide coverage, it has enough potential to meet the requirements of a like wise course of other Universities.

For the preparation of this text, the authors have taken help from the writings of many scholars. Their work has been constantly inspired by many of their students and colleagues. The authors feel a deep sense of gratitude to all of them.

What has been presented in the present text may appear a reiteration of what has been effectively said in some already existing publications covering various aspects of this text. However, as happens, every writer has his or her style and way of presentation. The present text, accordingly differs much in many ways with some of its features highlighted as under:

- It covers each and every aspect of the prescribed syllabus quite in detail.
- The language and style of presentation is well with in the capacity and likings of the readers.
- Appropriate questions (both essay type and short answer type) have been provided for the recapitulation exercise as well as meeting the needs of evaluation task at the end of the text in the student edition.
- Up-to-date references and suggestions for further study in the matter related to each and every chapter have also been given at the end of the text for serving the desired needs of students as well as teacher educators.

It is hoped, that in its present form, the text will prove beneficial to those for whom it is intended. Any suggestions for its improvement will be highly appreciated and thankfully acknowledged.

With good wishes to its readers.

20th May, 2017

S.K. Mangal
Shubhra Mangal

Contents

1

Measurement, Assessment, Evaluation and Evaluation Approaches

Introduction

The process of teaching and learning in one or the other subjects of the school curriculum always works for the realization of the stipulated teaching-learning objectives by following a well thought programme. Here also a teacher while adopting a definite curriculum and methodology of teaching strives hard for the achievement of the desired aims and objectives of teaching within the specific time period. In his way, meanwhile he naturally becomes eager to know about the results of his striving either for providing necessary magnitude and direction to the ongoing, teaching-learning process or for taking some or the other educational and administrative decisions in the interest of his students. For doing so he however needs some specific information related to the nature of the realization of the set teaching-learning objectives and individual achievements of his students in terms of the expected behavioural changes. In this task he is more often helped by the data derived through the means like test, measurement, assessment and evaluation. Let us know about these so used terms for providing needed information to the teachers to take necessary educational and administrative decisions.

Concept of Test, Measurement and Evaluation

You may have heard or undergone through the instruments like achievement tests, aptitude tests, intelligence tests, etc. Each of these instruments consists of a standard set of questions needed to be answered by you. On the basis of responses given by you, we obtain a measure/score *i.e.* a numerical value of the characteristic possessed by you in relation to your performance in a subject, intelligence or aptitude, etc. In this way you can understand a test simply as a measuring instrument consisting of a standard set of questions for being answered by the individual student with regard to one or the other characteristics of his behaviour. Mind that the use of the term 'test' is only limited to the use of some or the other specific set of questions and 'testing' as a process of making the students answer that set of questions. Upto this extent no process or act of measurement is involved. It begins with the work of assigning numbers to the test results according to a specific rule like counting correct answers and assigning one mark each for every correct answer.

Measurement in this way is a one step ahead of the process of testing. When the work of testing ends, measurement comes into picture for assigning numerical values to the test results. However, the process of measurement does not necessarily rest on tests and testing. It is quite a broader concept. Both testing (like achievement tests and intelligence may be used in the process of measuring a characteristic, i.e., obtaining information in a quantitative form. We may derive scores or obtain numerical description of the degree to which you as an individual possess a particular characteristic. In this way how much potential you possess in a particular aspect of your behaviour {i.e., knowledge, understanding, skills and applications of mathematical facts and principles, etc.) may be adjudged quantitatively with the help of the product and process of measurement. Let us make the meaning of term measurement more clear with the following definitions:

Carter V. Good: Measurement may be understood as "the comparison of a quantity (exhibited in a particular case) with an appropriate scale for the purpose of determining (within the limits of accuracy imposed by the nature of the scale) the numerical value on the scale that corresponds to the quantity to be measured."— (1959, pp. 337-38)

Remmers, Gaze and Rummel: Measurement refers to observations that can be expressed quantitatively and answers the question "how much."— (1960, pp. 7-8)

Mahesh Bhargava: "Measurement is the process of assigning symbols or numerals to observations, objects or events in some meaningful or consistent manner according to rule." — (1987, p. 53)

Gronlund and Linn: The term measurement is limited to quantitative description of pupils; that is, the results of measurement are always expressed in numbers (e.g. Mary correctly solves 35 out of the total 40 arithmetic problems). It does not include qualitative descriptions (Mary's work was neat) nor does it imply judgement concerning the worth or value of the obtained results.—(1990, p. 6)

The analysis of above definitions may clearly reveal that measurement is nothing by a process of quantification, *i.e.*, assigning units of measurements or numeral values to the types of characteristics observed in the behaviour or nature of an individual or object during some observation or testing. For example, when we say that the height of an individual is 160 centimetres or his score on a unit test of mathematics is 8 (correctly answered 8 out of the 10 objectives type questions), we are definitely resorting to the process measurement. A centimetre and score of one both here represent the respective units of measurement and the individuals are assigned different units on the basis of the performance exhibited by them during observation or testing. In fact, we try to assign numeral values or express the results of our observations or testing in a quantitative term through the process of measurement as precisely and objectively as possible.

Now coming to evaluation, we will soon realise that it is a quite comprehensive and broader term than measurement and testing. A glimpse of the following definitions may reveal the meaning and nature of the term evaluation.

Carter V. Good: Evaluation is the process of ascertaining or judging the value or amount of something by use of a standard of appraisal.
—(1959, p. 209)

Stufflebeam and others: "Evaluation is the process of delineating, obtaining and providing useful information for Judging decision alternatives."—(1971, p. 25)

Remmers, Gage and Rummel: "Evaluation is not just a testing programme. Tests are but one of many different techniques such as observation, checklists, questionnaires, interviews etc. that may contribute to the total evaluation programme."—(1960, p. 6)

Wright Stone: "Evaluation is relatively new technical term introduced to designate a more comprehensive concept of measurement that is applied in conventional tests and examination .... the emphasis is upon broad personality changes and major objectives of educational programme. These include not only subject matter achievements but also attitudes, interests, ideals, ways of thinking, work habits and personal and social adaptability."—(1956, p. 8)

Torgerson and Adams: "To evaluate is to ascertain the value of a process or a thing. Thus educational evaluation is the passing of judgement on the degree of worthwhileness of a teaching process or learning experience." — (1955, p. 5)

Ahmann and Glock: "Educational evaluation is a process in which a teacher commonly uses information derived from many sources in order to arrive at a value judgement. The information might be obtained by using measuring instruments as well as other techniques, direct observation and interviews. An evaluation may or may not be based upon measurement data, though appropriate measurement results are customarily used if they are available. Thus evaluation includes not only measuring or in some way identifying the degree to which a pupil possesses a trait or the degree of which a pupil's behaviour may have been modified as a result of a educational experience, but also judging the desirability and adequacy of these findings." — (1959, p. 13)

Indian Education Commission (1966): "It is now agreed that evaluation is a continuous process, forms an integral part of the total system of education and is ultimately related to educational objectives. It exercises a great influence on the pupil's educational achievements but also improves it."

Quillen and Hanna: "Evaluation is the process of gathering and interpreting evidences on change in the behaviour of the students as they progress through school."

An analysis of the above definitions may clearly reveal the following facts about the nature and characteristics of the term evaluation.

- Evaluation is more comprehensive term than measurement or testing.
- It represents a continuous process and overall efforts for knowing about the progress of the learner.
- It provides quantitative as well as qualitative description of the outcomes of teaching-learning process.
- It helps in knowing about the changes in behaviour related to the domains of the learner's behaviour as a result of the process of teaching-learning.
- It provides greater scope and flexibility for the use of variety of means and techniques rather than limiting itself to certain tests or conventional examinations.
- It represents a comprehensive plan of better testing and measurement for inquiring into the quality of the output in the light of the set objectives.
- It provides sufficient value judgement about the progress of the learner, teacher's efforts and effectiveness of the instructional programmes.

How Evaluation Differs from Measurement?

From the description given above we can easily conclude that evaluation is quite a wider and more comprehensive term than measurement. The differences between them particularly in the field of teaching and learning can be further emphasized as below:

1. The term measurement is limited to the quantitative descriptions of the potential and achievements of pupils, *i.e.,* the results of measurement are always expressed in numbers (*e.g.*, Ramesh's score on an achievement test is 60 out of the total 100 marks). Here no qualitative descriptions like neatness of his work, originality in the solution of the problems, etc. are mentioned. Evaluation, on the other hand, may include both quantitative descriptions (measurement) and qualitative description (non-measurement) of the pupils. Therefore, the changes in behaviour of the pupils that can be expressed in quantitative terms may only be ascertained through measuring devices. But where expression of the outcomes is available in the qualitative terms, measurement fails to convey the results. It is why the changes in the areas like interests, attitudes, habits, temperament, personal and social adjustment, etc. cannot be measured as absolutely as may happen in the measurement of the acquisition of skill and information, related to the conative and cognitive domains of the learners's behaviour. The changes in the affective domain (assessed through non-measuring techniques) can thus be made a subject of

evaluation and not of the measurement. In this way, if we need a comprehensive evaluation of the growth and development of the pupils in all the dimensions and domains of their personality and behaviour we have to go beyond the use of measurement and adopt evaluation techniques.

2. However, the most important and essential feature and distinction between the two terms evaluation and measurement lies with regard to the inclusion and non-inclusion of value judgements in their functioning. Measurement while limited to the quantitative description of the attributes of the pupils never tries to pass value attributes judgements over the measured attributes like good, bad, satisfactory, unsatisfactory, etc. For example, it may declare that Sheela has got 60% marks in a mathematics test but it will not pass any value judgement over the worth or value of her getting so much marks. In this way where measurement is limited to provide answer to the question how much is the achievement of a pupil, evaluation goes a step further to pass value judgement over the quantitative expressions derived through measurement. While evaluating, thus a teacher will definitely pass value judgement over the quantity expressed as 60%. He will provide division or grading and will consider her achievement as satisfactory, unsatisfactory, desirable or undesirable according to the individuality and needs of the teaching-learning situations.

3. In the process of evaluation value judgements are passed over the desirability of the results irrespective of their nature (being derived through measurement or non-measurement techniques.) Hence, while resorting to evaluation teacher may pass value judgement over getting 60% marks in an achievement test (involving measurement techniques) or interpret the results of a simple observation, interview encounter and rating scale grading for considering the value or goodness of the performance exhibited by a individual student. It is implied therefore that where measurement automatically falls into the domain of evaluation, it is not at all essential for the product and process of evaluation to depend upon the mercy of any quantification or measurement of the attributes of a pupil for passing judgement, over the worthwhileness of his progress and potentiality during a teaching-learning process, *i.e.,* bringing modification in his behaviour through any piece of formal or informal instruction.

4. Summing in this way we may easily conclude about the comprehensiveness and wideness of the term evaluation over measurement in the following ways:

(i) Evaluation may depend upon the results of measurement but goes a step further for passing judgement over the measured results, *i.e.,* interpretation and worthwhileness of 60% marks according to the given circumstances.

(ii) Evaluation may depend upon the results of non-measurement or testing device like observation, rating and interviews, etc. for passing out the judgement of their worthwhileness in a given situation.

(iii) Evaluation may include both quantitative description (measurement) and qualitative descriptions (non-measurement) of pupils for passing value judgement over the worthwhileness of their progress.

The above cited comprehensive nature of evaluation in relation to the involvement of measurement techniques (quantitative descriptions) and non-measurement techniques (qualitative descriptions) may be properly depicted through the following relationships.

(i) Evaluation = Quantitative descriptions of the progress (measurement) + value judgement.

(ii) Evaluation = Qualitative descriptions of the progress (non-measurement) + value judgement.

(iii) Evaluation = Quantitative + Qualitative descriptions of the progress (measurement and non-measurement) + value judgement.

All the above three relationships may be further illustrated through a single flow diagram depicted as under.

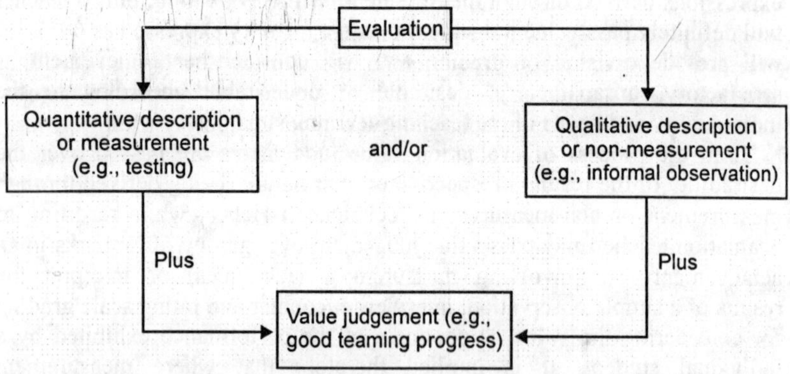

Fig. 1.1: Comprehensive Nature of Evaluation

Source: Gronlund and Linn, 1990, p. 6.

Concept of Examinations

Every one of use is very much acquainted with the use and application of the term examination. As a student you must have gone through a number of examinations while getting promoted from one grade to another or seeking admission to academic classes and professional courses by crossing the barriers of entrance examinations. In a course of a year while studying in a particular grade, you may have faced a compulsion of appearing in the terminal, half yearly or annual examination for enabling you to be declared as passed in that grade. In fact what we term as examination is an age old concept use for measuring the achievement or performance level of the students well after a specified time measuring the achievement or performance areas determined by the curriculum or syllabus of a particular grade or school stage (*i.e.* elementary, Secondary or higher secondary). The term examination has been under attack on one or the other accounts and have now been almost replaced by the term evaluation.

Distinction between Examination and Evaluation

In practice many times these two terms are used interchangeably. But in spite of the fact that both aim at the same thing or things, they differ in so many ways. Evaluation is relatively a new term in the field of education. It has a more extensive scope and is definitely more valid, objective and purposeful than examination. The relative difference can be summarized as under:

Examination	*Evaluation*
1. It refers to a system where students are tested just at the end of a definite period of instruction.	1. The changes brought in the behaviour of the students through education are continuous. Evaluation helps in the continuous appraisal of such changes.
2. It limits itself to the testing of knowledge and skills of subject matter.	2. Through evaluation it is possible to test the overall changes brought in the behaviour and personality of the children.

Concept of Assessment

We use the term assessment in various ways in our day-to-day life such as assessment of the rental value of a building, assessment of the property tax on a house, internal assessment of the achievements and performances of the students, quality assessment of a thing or person, etc. In saying so, we often mean to have a proper value judgement or worth of a thing, person or process. The quantitative as well as qualitative aspects of its worth are very much involved in doing assessment of a thing or process. Decidedly in this way the term assessment is more comprehensive than the term measurement. While having assessment of a house we have to take consideration of the number of rooms, quality of the material used in its construction, the type of flooring and roofing, its furnishing and type of facilities available in the form of electricity, ventilations, modular kitchen, toilets and bath room, hall and garden, etc. Here, thus, we would like to use quantifying terms as well as qualifying terms while providing assessment report of this house. The same will also happen when we would be asked to provide the assessment report of a students or self-assessment report of our own as teacher/employer of the school. While preparing assessment reports of the hockey team in our charge we have to assess the work of each player of the team in quantitative as well as qualitative terms, *e.g.* average time devoted in practice, attendance in the field, number of penalties committed in the practice and competition matches, the goals scored or allowed, etc.

In the field of education the term assessment in reference to the searching or judging of the achievements or performances of the students is very much utilized as to take a wholesome consideration about the value or worth of a particular student by making use of quantitative and qualitative description of his/her achievement and performances regarding a particular course of learning during a specified time.

In case, we try to compare the use of the terms assessment and evaluation in reference to the screening or passing value judgement over the work or quality of the performances shown by the students in a particular learning field we may come to realize that both aim and mean for the same. It is why, the term assessment and evaluation are used interchangeably much like as the synonyms terms.

Distinction between Assessment of Learning and Assessment for Learning

Assessment of Learning

The term Assessment of Learning stands for a type of assessment task carried out for assessing the learning or behavioural outcomes of the learners after the execution of a learning activity, schedule or programme. The main characteristics of such type of assessment, may be outlined as below:

1. Through such type of assessment, we try to assess:
   (i) How good or bad a learning has been shaped or occurred as a result of the on going learning efforts?
   (ii) How far the learning objectives set for a particular piece of learning have been achieved?
   (iii) What type of changes or modifications in the behaviour of the learners are visible as a result of learning?
2. It stands for the net result or outcomes of a learning process accessible through a net difference between learning output of the terminal behaviour and initial input or entry behaviour, *i.e.,* Assessment of Learning = Learning potential at the end of a learning process – (minus) Learning potential at the beginning of the learning process
3. It is carried out strictly at the end of a learning to get acquainted the learners with the fruits of their learning efforts.
4. It can take the shape of a formative or summative assessment depending upon the time and schedule adopted for assessing the learning outcomes of the learners. When it is undertaken well after the finishing of a course, semester or otherwise after a fixed duration then it can take the form of a summative assessment. However, when the process of assessment or evaluation is turned into a continuous process of assessing the learning outcomes of the students, then it results into a type of assessment known as formative assessment.

Here we try to have assessment of the learning outcomes of a learner quite frequently, time to time for having a full check and control over the learning process and output of a learner.

Assessment for Learning

The term assessment for learning stands for a type of assessment task carried out for accessing the existing potential of a student or learner to as ascertain how far s/he is capable of learning a given task. The output of such assessment makes the task of a learner or teacher to learn or teach a particular piece of learning quite easy and methodological. Based upon this input s/he may plan for his journey of learning or teaching in a proper form. The nature of this type of assessment is characterized with the features like below:

1. It is carried out well before undertaking or executing a task of learning.
2. The decision about undertaking a learning task is carried out in the light of the results derived from such type of assessment.
3. A teacher tries to resort to such type of assessment in the form of testing the previous knowledge of his/her students regarding the teaching-learning of a particular topic well before the presentation of the subject matter related to that topic to the class. S/he plans her/his methodology and delivery of the lesson by getting insight from the result of the previous knowledge testing, *i.e.*, a typical form of assessment for learning.
4. The feedback received through the tests and measures like IQ and EQ testing, aptitude test, interest inventory, personality inventory, temperament and moods recognition tools may work as an effective input in the form of assessment for learning. What type of learning is suitable for a particular type of learners, may be properly undertaken in the light of the feedback received through such assessment. The decision about the methodology employed, devices and aid material used etc. is also undertaken for carrying out a learning process in the light of such feedback.
5. What we know as a diagnostic assessment or testing can be very well termed an assessment for learning. Through such assessment or testing we try to diagnose or identify the learning difficulties, strength and weaknesses of a learner in relation to the learning of a particular task, topic or subject area. The feedback received from such diagnosis then can help in planning for and undertaking a learning task remedial in nature for helping the learner in getting rid of his learning difficulties. Removal of such hurdles in the path of learning may facilitate the task of further learning and in this way diagnostic testing or assessment can successfully assume the role of assessment for learning.

6. In formative assessment, we try to assess the learning of a learner time to time to test or assess his/her progress on the learning path. Such assessment at one or the other stage of a learning process may play well the role of "assessment for learning" since it acquaints the learner with his/her readiness or potential for further learning with sufficient knowledge of any deficiency, short-comings or difficulties in his/her path of learning. Such feedback may help the learner in planning and organising task of further learning in a desirable way.

In this way assessment for learning may be carried out in a variety of mode by adopting one or the other means. However, in all its forms and shapes its nature and purpose always remains totally formative, *i.e.*, helping or preparing a learner for undertaking one or the other learning task for its execution in a proper way.

Needs and Objectives of Assessment or Evaluation

The function served and fruits realised through the process of evaluation may help us to lay down, the objectives or identify the needs of evaluation in the manner given below:

1. To help in laying out or bringing modification in the instructional and educational objectives of teaching for a particular grade in a specified teaching-learning situation.
2. To help in the selection and organisation of learning experiences for the teaching related to a particular grade and teaching-learning situation.
3. To help in the selection and use of general and specific teaching-learning strategies and methods for the teaching of specific topics and branches of the subjects in a particular grade and teaching-learning situation.
4. To help in diagnosing the learning difficulties of the students (general and specific) and accordingly plan suitable remedial teaching.
5. To help the teacher for better planning and organisation of his teaching task according to the needs of his students and prevailing teaching-learning situations.
6. To help the teachers and students for getting due incentives and motivation (extrinsic as well as intrinsic) for carrying out their teaching-learning functions.
7. To help the guidance and counselling personnel for providing educational, personal and vocational guidance and counselling to the needy students.
8. To help in the process of realization of the teaching-learning objectives of teaching to a particular grade in a given teaching-learning situation.
9. To help the teachers, students, parents, guidance personnel, administrators, curriculum framers, researchers and planners to take

needed decisions in their respective field of work in the light of the results of evaluation.

Scope or Functions of Assessment or Evaluation

The scope or functions served by the process of assessment or evaluation may be outlined as below.

1. Placement Function: The assessment or evaluation of the learning outcomes, abilities or performances of the students helps in one or the other types of placement activities in the manner like below:

(i) Evaluation data help in taking decision about the selection or placement of the students in a particular academic or professional course available in a particular educational institution.

(ii) These may also be used for the selection and placement of the students for the particular hobby or participation in co-curricular activities, including games and sports.

2. Feedback and Informational Functions: Assessment or evaluation data may be successfully used for providing useful, feedback and information to the concerned personnel in order to maintain the essential communicational channel in the process of teaching-learning like below:

(i) It may provide a good *feedback to the students* by constantly informing them about their progress (strengths and weaknesses) and level of performance concerning their learning efforts.

(ii) It may also provide sufficient *feedback to the teachers* in terms of the functionability and effectiveness of their models and strategies of teaching.

(iii) The outcomes of the valuation in the form of test scores, grades, stars, certificates, report cards, comments and remarks of the teachers provide *unique information to the parents* about the progress of their children. Such information is quite valuable for the welfare of the child firstly because he may get desired help and assistance from his parents for his educational progress and developmental needs and secondly for reinforcing his learning behaviour and keep him motivating outside the boundary walls of the school.

(iv) Evaluation data may also provide *necessary information to the school personnel* other than the teachers connected with the evaluation task. They can know much about the learning potential, abilities and capacities, interests and attitudes of a child concerning the different learning areas and in turn may help the child in his proper growth and development.

(v) Evaluation data provide information to the school administrators and educational authorities about the progress and functioning of the teaching-learning activities. Based on such communication, they may be able to exercise proper control over the working of the school in their charge.

(vi) Evaluation data may provide valuable information about the working and functioning of a school to the general public. Many a time, school's reputation is associated with the shining of its students in public or state examinations and competitions.

(vii) Evaluation results may also help in fixing responsibilities and accountability for the poor performance of the students with regards to their needed development in a particular area or subject.

3. Certification, Grading and Promotion functions: Evaluation or assessment data may be properly used for serving the functions like below.

(i) For providing certificates to the students certifying that a particular student has passed a learning course, standard or school/public examination by mentioning its scores, quality of performance and place in the class, district or state.

(ii) It may help in Grading (like A+, A, B, etc.) of the students for telling his or her standing with regard to his performance or achievement in the scholastic or non-scholastic areas.

(iii) It may help in promoting a student in the next senior class, level or standard of his learning/education. It may also help the teachers and school administrators in choosing the captain of a team, monitor of a class and leading boy or girl in cultural and social activities.

4. Diagnostic Functions: Evaluation or assessment data may also help in the diagnosis of learning difficulties of the students in various scholastic and non-scholastic areas. Based on such diagnosis then suitable steps can be taken for

(i) the organization of guidance and counselling programmes to the needy students.

(ii) the organization of special or remedial education to the needy children in relation to their learning difficulties.

5. Planning Functions: Assessment or evaluation data may also be properly used for exercising the following functions related with the planning of the teaching-learning tasks.

- It may help in the formulation of the set objectives for carrying out the teaching-learning tasks.
- It may help in the selection and organisation or appropriate learning experiences, framing syllabus and developing curriculum.
- The methods and strategies of teaching-learning, the aid material used etc. can be properly planned in view of the evaluation outcomes.
- Remedial teaching, individual teaching and group activities, special educational programmes can be better planned in the light of the evaluation outcomes.

6. Motivational Functions: The knowledge of the results and progress (provided by the process of assessment or evaluation) may prove a quite potent factor for motivating an individual to continue his efforts in the right direction. The evaluation measures help in acquainting the learners as well as teachers about the outcomes of their efforts and this in turn may prove a good incentive for keeping them on the teaching-learning track. In addition to this, evaluation data is quite often used for providing proper incentive to the students as well as teachers in the form of appreciation, grades, stickers, comments, division, certificate, etc. Such incentives play a dual role firstly to motivate the individual who receives such incentives and secondly to others who take it a challenge for working effectively to get such incentives.

Evaluation or Assessment Approaches

Evaluation or assessment of the process and outcome of learning involve the use of two approaches namely: (i) Formative, and (ii) Summative.
Let us discuss these approaches one by one.

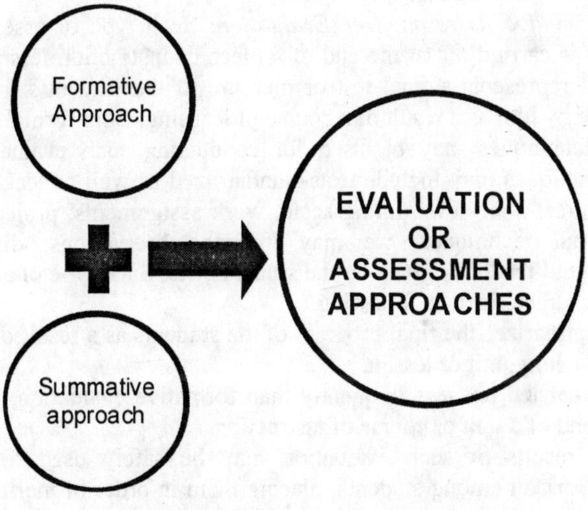

Fig. 1.2: Evaluation or Assessment Approaches

(i) Formative Assessment or Evaluation: This type of assessment or evaluation is conducted well during the teaching learning process. When a teacher has taught some content or some unit or provided some learning experience, he has a need to determine the outcome. Similarly, students also need to know about their progress in the path of learning. The formative evaluation helps in this task by providing useful information to both teacher and students about the strengths and weaknesses of their teaching and learning. In the light of this information, they may plan and engage for the mid course corrections in pace or content and methodology of instruction. The formative evaluation may be carried out both in formal (like checklists, quizzes, question-answers, assignments and tests) as well as informal (like observations, listening to students comments and conversations) way. The essential characteristics of such assessment may be briefly summarized as under.

- It is administered during the lesson taught or instruction imparted.
- It helps in informing the students about their progress chiefly about the amount they have yet to learn before achieving the set objectives.
- It is useful to the extent it remains informative, closely related to the things being taught, timely and frequent.
- It helps the teacher by providing him qualitative and quantitative data for bringing necessary modification in his teaching.
- It proves very useful in guiding the students, planning remedial instruction and prompting them to ask for necessary help.
- It should in no way be used by the teacher and the students, just as for making comparison among the students or making a certifying judgement. The results of such assessment should not necessarily appear in any official record.

(ii) Summative Assessment or Evaluation: Such type of assessment or evaluation is carried out at the end of a piece of instruction lesson or unit. Actually it represents a final test or measure of the student's progress or gains made by him as a result of a course of learning. Both formal as well as informal techniques may be used for conducting such evaluation. The formal techniques may include tests-standardized as well as teacher made, questionnaires, interviews, rating scale, work assignments, projects etc. In the informal techniques, we may include observations, discussions, comments and feedback given by the students, etc. Such type of assessment is chiefly characterized as following.

- It summarizes the final progress of the students as a result of a course of teaching unit or lesson.
- It is carried out less frequently than formative evaluation, usually at the end of a unit or course of instruction.
- The results of such evaluation may be safely used for making comparison among students, placing them in order of merit or taking decisions about their promotion and awarding degree or diploma. It is this characteristic of summative evaluation which enables it to be called as certifying evaluation.

2

Continuous and Comprehensive Evaluation (CCE)

What is Continuous and Comprehensive Evaluation or CCE?

Evaluation is a very essential part of any teaching-learning process as it forms the basis for feedback about the extent of success or failure of any teaching-learning situation.

Recently, a new form of Evaluation termed as Continuous and Comprehensive Evaluation (CCE) has come into practice in the school education. Let us understand in a brief overview as to what is meant by CCE and how is it different from the conventional evaluation and its meaning.

CCE makes evaluation an inherent part and parcel of the teaching-learning process. It aims at enhancement of learning through diagnosis and remediation. The two fold objectives of CCE are continuity in evaluation and assessment of broad learning and behavioural outcomes in a comprehensive way.

This system of evaluation, infact was very much emphasized in our National Education Policy-1986. Under the head "The Evaluation Process and Examination Reforms". Here it has been clearly laid down that there is a need of re-casting the examination system and to have provision for the system of "continuous and comprehensive evaluation that incorporates both scholastic and non-scholastic aspects of education, spread over the total span of the instructional time."

Accordingly the system of continuous and comprehensive evaluation has been incorporated by almost all of the boards of school education of the country. Taking the lead in this pursuit CBSE has clarified the concept of CCE in its manual (2009) in the manner given below:

> *Continuous and comprehensive evaluation (CCE) refers to a system of school-based evaluation of students that covers all aspects of students development. It is a development process of assessment which emphasizes on twofold objectives. These objectives are continuity in evaluation and assessment of broad-based learning and behavioural out comes on the other.*

While explaining the term continuity the manual says that the assessment of the students development is not a single time job but a task being carried put continuously throughout the session. Continuity of evaluation thus requires for system to (i) Introducing regularity in assessment (ii) increase in the number of unit tests. (iii) diagnose the learning deficiencies (iv) adopt remedial measures, (v) arrange for retesting and then (v) making use of the feedback for the self evaluation on the part of students and teachers. Regarding comprehensiveness of the evaluation, manual tells to make evaluation necessary comprehensive and complete quite capable of measuring and assessing the scholastic as well as non-scholastic achievements/performances of the students' development.

Regarding *what should be assessed and how*, the manual has pointed out the following:

1. The continuous and comprehensive evaluation of the learning outcomes of the students in all the three behavioural domains-cognitive, conative and affective.
2. The continuous and comprehension evaluation of the development of the students in all the dimensions of personality-physical, mental, social, emotional, moral and spiritual, artistic and aesthetic, creative and constructive etc.
3. The continuous and comprehensive evaluation of the performance in scholastic and non-scholastic areas (through the curricular as well as co-curricular activities) by making use of two types of evaluation formative and summative.
4. Adoption of suitable ways and means of evaluation capable of providing quantitative as well as qualitative assessment of the behavioural changes or learning achievements of the students in both the scholastic or non-scholastic areas such as outlined below:
   - Learning achievements in the knowledge area related to school subjects
   - Learning achievements related to practical and applied aspects of the school subjects.
   - Achievements/performance level in the participation of co-curricular activities
   - The acquisition level in various skills like thinking skills constructive and creative skills emotional skills, social and adaptive skills, life saving skills, civic and democratic living skill, etc.

The Need and Importance of CCE

The question arises, why this system of evaluation known as continuous and comprehensive evaluation should be incorporated in our system of education? The answer of this question is very much based in a subsequent question, after all what is the need of maintaining continuity and comprehensives in a scheme of evaluation? Let us think over this issue.

Continuity of Evaluation, Why?

By all means, we try to go through a process of evaluation to get aware of the results of the teaching-learning process, *i.e.,* the planned changes in the behaviour of the students. The changes occurring in the cognitive, conative and affective domains of the pupil's behaviour are non-stopping and continuous. They may occur at any time well in the duration of a teaching-learning process or academic session. A teacher may notify these changes even through a simple observation or interaction with the students in the situations involving scholastic and co-scholastic aspects of students' growth and development. In case he does not take notice of these changes and neglects the needed evaluation, he will be committing a cardinal educational error. It is good from every angle to have evaluation of the concomitant changes, in the behaviour of the pupils as a result of the process of teaching and learning as early and often as possible to provide proper feedback for improving the input, process and output of the instructional and educational systems well in tune with the philosophy of "system approach" adopted in Educational Technology (ET). It is necessary, therefore, on the part of a teacher to maintain proper continuity in the use of evaluation device for keeping the teaching-learning process on a proper track for the realization of the set teaching-learning objectives, diagnosing the learning gaps, difficulties and weaknesses of the learners and teaching-learning system and then introduce timely remedies in the overall welfare of the students.

In the traditional system of evaluation termed as examination we had the provision of examination conducted at the fixed intervals of time *i.e.* half yearly, or yearly examination etc. We could know about the strengths and weaknesses of the students only after a fixed period of time. Imagine a situation that after a lapse of one full year, we come to know that a child is not doing well or failing miserably in a particular subject or subjects. However, what could be done now? Had we have known about his progress earlier, he could have been helped through some remedial action in getting through his weakness in a learning area. It is here thus the need of continuous evaluation is strongly felt and it is why Indian Education commission (1964-66) also strongly recommended to have proper provision of maintaining continuity in the evaluation of the performance of the students by commenting in the manner given below:

> "*It is now agreed that evaluation is a continuous process, forms an integral part of the total system of education and is ultimately related to educational objectives. It exercises a great influence on the pupil's study habits and the teacher's method of instruction and thus helps not only to measure educational achievements but also improves it.*"

Comprehensive of Evaluation, Why?

Evaluation of the learning outcomes of the pupils is chiefly carried out to pass value judgement over the nature of the changes occurring in the behaviour of the students through curricular and co-curricular experiences provided to the learners. Since changes in behaviour are brought out in all the aspects of one's behaviour-cognitive, conative and affective resulting in one's overall growth and development in all the dimensions of his/her personality, it makes a strong plea to take all of them in consideration while making assessment or evaluating the outcome of a teaching learning process. We must be quite capable of assessing the progress of the students towards the wholesome development of their personality. The traditional system of examination is not capable of measuring behavioural changes occurring in all the domains of behaviour. It also can't measure or assess the learning outcomes well in both the scholastic and non-scholastic areas in their totality. Therefore, there arises a need to adopt a system of comprehensive evaluation.

How to Carry on with the System of CCE

The necessity of making the task of evaluation as a continuous and comprehensive process has been responsible for introducing considerable changes in the methods, techniques and overall approach adopted in measuring and evaluating the learning outcomes and progress of the students.

In place of age old annual examination system or seasonal/half yearly examinations, the trend is now for adopting ways and means for carrying out continuous and comprehensive evaluation of outcome of the learning and achievements of the learners in the various domains of their behaviour and personality. It involves the use of multiple and comprehensive testing and non-testing tools and devices.

A formal scheme of CCE, asks for the use of two types of evaluation known as formative evaluation and summative evaluation helpful in carrying out the evaluation in its needed continuity and comprehensiveness.

Formative evaluation is formative and constructive in nature. It is carried out well in the duration of the teaching-learning process for knowing about its outcomes in relation to the realization of the set teaching-learning objectives. It provides useful information to both the teachers and students about the strengths and weaknesses of their teaching and learning. In the light of this information, they may plan and engage for the mid-course corrections in their teaching and learning tasks.

Summative evaluation is carried out at the end of a piece of instruction of a lesson or unit. Actually it represents a final test or measure of the student's progress or gains made by him as a result of a course of learning.

In carrying out both of these evaluations-formative as well as summative, both formal as well as informal techniques like below are in general being used by the teachers in the name of evaluating the learning/behavioural outcomes of their students.

- The nature and quality of the responses of the students to the questions asked by the teacher in the class.
- The observation record of the behaviour of the students in the class,

laboratories, workshops and other places of curricular or co-curricular activities.

- The performance of the students in the drill and practice work given to the students in the class.
- Performance of the students in the practical and project work done in the school.
- The quality of the work done by the students in relation to given assignments and home tasks.
- Performance of the students in interviews or viva voice examination.
- Performance of the students in the periodical tests and examinations such as weekly and monthly tests and quarterly, half yearly or annual examinations.
- The responses received through the assessment tools like questionnaires, rating scales, check lists, attitude scales, interest inventories, adjustment inventories and personality measures.
- Performance in the standardized diagnostic as well as achievement tests available in the areas and units of different school subjects.

Problems faced by teachers in the implementation of CCE

There is no doubt that the scheme of continuous and comprehensive evaluation (CCE) caters well for the needed progress and development of the students in a quite appropriate way and therefore should be accepted and implemented by the schools in a quite sincere and appropriate way. However, there is a possibility of its half-heartedly acceptance or improper implementation at the hands of teachers and school authorities on account of a number of problems faced by them in its proper implementation. The types of problems usually felt on this account can be summarized as below:

1. The meaning, nature, concept, objective and way of its implementation is not properly clear to the teachers or account of the lack of proper orientation and training in this concern.

2. The prevailing environment and the attitude of the parents, students, school administration and general public is not favourable towards the implementation of CCE. The traditional pattern of over emphasis on the scholastic areas and competition for the merit positions or overall improvement in the pass percentage rules the teaching-learning environment prevailed and practices employed in the schools. Since no proper weightage is given to the students' wholesome growth and development and achievement in non-scholastic areas, the need of carrying out continuous and comprehensive evaluation is not seriously realized. With such apathy shown towards the implementation of CCE on the part of stakeholders, it is becoming a uphill task for the teachers to raise the flag of CCE in the schools.

3. It needs a lot of time, resources and energy to carry out continuous and comprehensive evaluation of the learning outcomes and performances of the students in all the scholastic and non-scholastic areas of the school

curriculum. The assessment of learning outcomes and behaviour changes in all the domains-cognitive, conative and affective need to employ a variety of methods, tools and techniques, appropriately designed and suited to the learning and developmental needs of the students. The use and application of such diversified means of assessment becomes a tedious problem and challenge to the school teachers. They have no sufficient knowledge and skills of applying and using these tools and techniques. The cooperation from the school authorities in terms of the needed facilities and resources is also not easily available to them. Students are not also prepared and used to the employment of such assessment tools and techniques and parents do not feel the need of such assessment. Teachers also complain about getting little time for devoting their energy in the proper organization of scholastic and non-scholastic activities and their evaluation properly in the spirit of the CCE scheme. All these things are standing in the way of teachers for making their determined efforts towards the implementation of CCE.

3

Tools and Technique of Evaluation

Introduction

Tools and Techniques of assessment or evaluation represent those ways and means which help measure and assess the teaching-learning outcomes, *i.e.* to know the extent to which the desired behavioural changes have taken place in the learner. These changes, both quantitative as well as qualitative, occur in all the three domains — cognitive, conative and affective — of the behaviour of the learner. The teachers make use of so many formal and informal techniques for the measurement and assessment of the teaching-learning outcomes, which include:

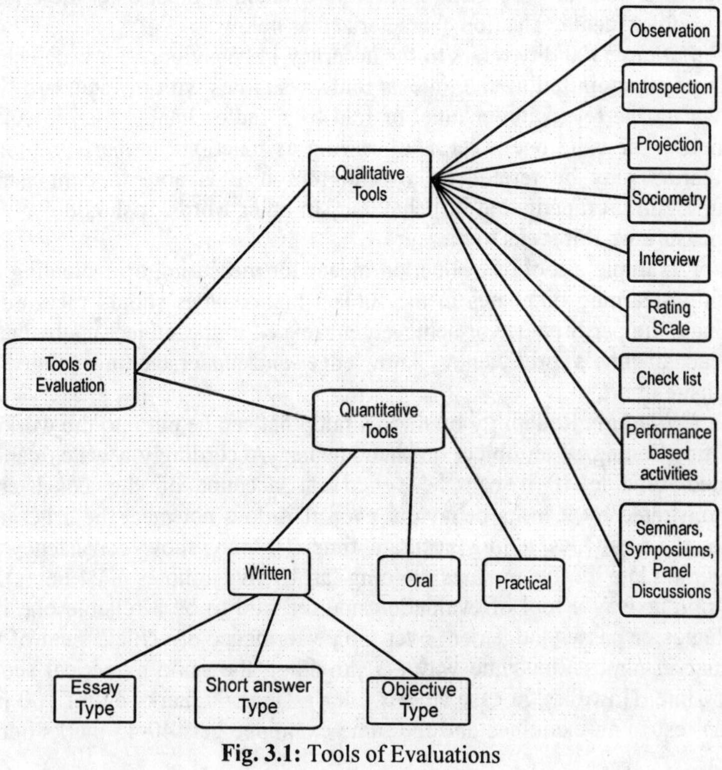

Fig. 3.1: Tools of Evaluations

(a) Oral tests and examinations.
(b) Practical tests and examinations.
(c) Written tests and examinations consisting of essay, and objective and short answer type questions.
(d) Tools and techniques such as observations introspection, projection, sociometry, discussion, questionnaire, inventory, interview, checklist, attitude scale, rating scale, case study, etc.

In this chapter we would like to have discussion on a few important tools and techniques employed for the quantitative and qualitative evaluation of the learning outcomes of the students. However, before discussing about these evaluation tools let us first consider the criteria used for naming an evaluation tool as an ideal tool.

Characteristics of a Good Measuring Instrument or Tool of Evaluation

Evaluation is a quite essential element or component of the teaching-learning process or the education system in general. It can help well in serving the interests and ends of learners, teachers, parents, school administers, educational planners, employers and others associated with the processes and products of education. However, for serving its purposes well a system or tool of the measurement and evaluation must meet the criteria of a good or ideal evaluation characterized as below:

1. *Validity*: Validity refers to the accuracy in behaviour. If a watch show quite accuracy in telling the time as it always tallies with the standard time shown on the television channel or told by a radio channel then it can be termed as the valid one in terms of serving its function. Similarly, a tool of evaluation may be termed as a valid tool if it is able to demonstrate accuracy in its functioning or behaviour. In other words, it should evaluate or measure what it seeks to measure.

For example a tool of evaluation meant for measuring or evaluating the teaching-learning outcomes in the subject mathematics should measure or evaluate the performance or achievement related to the subject mathematics instead of one's proficiency, knowledge and understanding related to language or art.

2. *Reliability*: Reliability refers to a faith that can be put into the working and functioning of an object or phenomenon. Accordingly a watch can be termed reliable if it can be relied on account of the consistency demonstrated by it in its behaviour even if it does not meet the criteria of validity *i.e.* always telling accurate time. (It may show consistency by remaining late by five minutes or going fast by five minutes in 24 hours). In the similar way a tool of evaluation may be said to be a reliable one if it evaluates or passes judgement over the performance or achievement of the learner in almost the same way *i.e.* providing the same numerical scores everytime. However, in case an evaluator assigns 60 marks out of 100 in a given test to an examinee and the same examinee gets 40-45 marks out of

100 if his answer book (the similar-one evaluated by the first examiner) are evaluated by the second examiner, then the test or evaluation tool can not be termed as a reliable one.

3. *Objectivity*: The evaluation is said to be objectives if responding to the test items on the part of the examinees or marking of the responses by the evaluators is not at all affected by their respective personal interests, attitudes, feelings and whims. In other words, subjectivity inherent or shown by the examinees and evaluators on their part in terms of fulfilling their duties as examinee and evaluator does not affect the evaluation outcomes in a tool then it is termed as objective. In this respect when the essay type examinations are loaded with extreme subjectivity on the part of examinees and evaluation, the objective type carries sufficient objectivity on account of having a single straight forward response for the items included in them. *e.g.* an item like who is responsible for the down fall of Mughal empire? May be coloured widely with the interests, attitudes, fund of knowledge, feelings and whims of both the examinees and evaluators. However an item like "Aurangzeb is most often blamed for the down fall of ... empire", may be termed as sufficiently objective.

4. Comprehensiveness: Comprehensiveness of a test or evaluation tool is known or estimated through the length of the test or the amount of its coverage of the assessment of the learning outcomes or achievements of the students. Accordingly a test or evaluation tool may be said to be quite comprehensive, if it demonstrates its capability of measuring or assessing the teaching-learning outcomes related with each and every aspect of the content material, topic or units of the subject covered through the classroom teaching-learning. In this way. a test or evaluation for being equipped with the characteristic of comprehensiveness need to have large number of questions for providing representation to the evaluation of what has been expected from the learners in terms of the teaching-learning outcomes. In this connection where essay type examinations may have less or no scope for demonstrating the quality of comprehensiveness, the test including short answer type or objective ones may demonstrate sufficient characteristics of comprehensiveness by including large number of questions and providing coverage to the wide area of contents and topics covered in a particular session.

5. *Diagnosticity*: A good evaluation tool is characterized with the quality of being diagnostic in nature. We know that a proper diagnosis is always needed for providing a proper cure or treatment to an ailment or disease. The same is true with the students suffering from the learning difficulties, inefficiency and failures. We must have a proper diagnosis of their difficulties and weaknesses related to their-learning areas or behavioural dimensions for getting rid of them with their-deficiencies and problems. Accordingly, a system or tool of evaluation must invariably help in supplying information related to such diagnosis.

6. *Practicability*: A good evaluation tool or test must be equipped with the features associated with the needed convenience and practicability of its construction and use in the manner given below:

(a) *Ease in preparation*: The evaluation tool or test should be quite convenient and economical in terms of labour, time and expenditure for its preparation and construction at the hands of the paper setters or tool developers.

(b) *Ease in Administration*: The evaluation tool or test should not pose unnecessary inconvenience or problems at the time of its administration *i.e.* taking examination or testing the students. More particularly, it should not pose the problems related to copying, talking or consulting with each other or temptation of knowing answer by hook and crook, etc.

(c) *Ease in scoring*: The evaluation tool or test should not pose difficulties or problems to the evaluators in evaluating the responses of the examinees. We can understand very well that the evaluation of the responses of the essay type questions may prove a big headache for the evaluators as it becomes difficult for providing fare and objective treatment for the lengthy responses of the wide variety of the examinees. On the other hand, the short answer or objective type questions may prove quite handy and convenient to them for their single and straight forward responses.

Establishing Reliability and Validity of the Test or Tools

Standardization of a test essentially requires on the part of the test developer the execution of the task related to the establishment of a reasonable degree of reliability and validity of his test.

The establishment of reliability and validity of the test, in fact, helps both the test developer and the publisher in winning the faith and trust of the users in the use of the test. It helps the researchers to get the necessary confidence in making use of the tool and derive the reliable and valid data with its use. In this way, it becomes quite beneficial as well as necessary on the part of the test developers to establish the reliability and validity of his tool for making its application safe as well as worthwhile to the population for whom it has been designed. The test developer for this purpose must be clear about the concepts of reliability and validity, their nature, types and methodology of their computation.

There are various types of test reliability like:

(i) test-retest reliability,

(ii) equivalent forms reliability (if two equivalent forms of the test are available), and

(iii) internal consistency (by making use of split-half method, KR20 or alpha coefficient) that may needed to be established by the test developer.

Similarly, he may need to establish the validity of his tool in a number of forms like:

(i) face validity,
(ii) content validity,
(iii) construct validity, and
(iv) criterion-related validity, depending on the precision required and purposes served through the use of the test.

Establishment of the Reliability of the Test

Reliability of a test refers to the faith and trust that can be put with the use of this test for evaluation/testing purpose on the part of users. There are a number of methods and techniques for the establishment of the reliability of a test or assessment tool. However, at present here we would like to discuss the two most common methods of establishing reliability of a test by the test developers. These are: (i) Test-retest method, and (ii) Split-half method. Let us know about them one by one.

Test-retest method: This is a commonly used method for establishing the reliability of an assessment tool. As the name suggests, the administration of the test needs repetition in the form of testing and re-testing for the estimation of its reliability. The steps employed for the use of this method may be outlined as below.

Step 1. Administer the test on a representative sample of the population.

Step 2. Administer the same test on the same sample under the same or similar condition within appropriate time span (neither too long nor too short).

Step 3. Compute the test-retest correlation coefficient between the scores of the test and retest.

Step 4. Try to interpret the reliability of your developed test in the light of the value of correlation coefficient derived in step 3. If it is significant, then you may get assured about the reliability of your test.

Use of split-half method: In making use of split-half method for establishing reliability of his test, the test developer has to split the test in two equal halves. Usually, for this purpose the odd-even procedure is employed.

In the odd-even split, a test developer administers his test at one time on the representative sample but scores the items of the test as though they are two separate tests in themselves. The steps involved in the use of this method involving odd-even split may be outlined as below:

Step 1: Administer the test on a representative sample of the population.

Step 2: Score the items of the test and tabulate the results in the two columns for each subject of the sample in the manner given below:

S. No. of the odd item	*Score of the odd item*	*S. No. of the even item*	*Score of the even item*
Item no.1	......	Item no.2	....
Item no. 3	....	Item no 4	....
Item no. 5	....	Item no.6	......
	Total score X		Total score Y

Step 3: Now tabulate the total scores earned by the individual subjects on the odd and even items in the manner given below.

Total score earned on odd items	Total score earned on even items
X_1	Y_1
X_2	Y_2
X_3	Y_3
X_4	Y_4

(Here X_1 stands for the total score earned by the subject No. 1 on the odd items and Y_1 stands for the score earned by him on the even items.)

Step 4: Now compute the correlation coefficient between the set of the scores X and Y. It will yield a correlation coefficient between the sets of odd and even scores known as split-half reliability coefficient. Let it be r_1

Step 5: Now estimate a reliability correlation coefficient for the whole test by making use of the Spearmen Brown Prophecy Formula given below.

$$r = 2r_1/(1 + r_1)$$

where r = Reliability correlation coefficient for the whole test and

r_1 = split-half reliability coefficient (the actual correlation between the halves of the test)

Establishing Validity of the Test

A test is said to be valid when it measures what it ought to measure. Therefore, the task of establishing the validity of a test is nothing but a way of ensuring that the developed test is going to measure all that for the measurement of which it has been designed by the test developer and employed by the users.

In establishing validity of the achievement tests, usually the test developers try to establish following three types of validity

1. Face Validity
2. Content Validity
3. Criterion related Validity

Let us know about them in brief.

Face Validity

Face validity, as its name suggests, is a type of validity of a test that is judged through its face value. We know that for terming a test valid, its items or questions should have a proper link with the objectives of the test. If it appears on a superficial inspection by the judges (including the test developer himself) that the items are helping in the establishment of this link (*i.e.,* helping in the realization of the objectives), then the test may be termed a valid test.

In this way, face validity of a test is nothing but a judgement concerning how relevant the test items appear to be just on the basis of their superficial inspection. Stated another way, if a test provides reasonable evidence through its appearance to measure what it supposed to measure "on the face of it", it could be said to be high in face validity.

Procedure Adopted for Establishing Face Validity

The test developer is needed to go ahead for the establishment of the face validity of his test in the manner given below.

1. First, he should approach a panel of judges (consisting of the experts and experienced persons related to the subject or area of the test) for helping in the establishment of the face validity of his tool. Besides this, he may also put himself in the position of an evaluator or judge for taking decision concerning the face validity of the tool.
2. After that, he should try to request the judges to initiate for the evaluation or judgement of the items of the test on their face value by keeping into consideration the things like below for this purpose:
   (i) Does the instrument appear to you measuring what it needs to measure?
   (ii) Does each item of the test appear to contribute towards the realization of objectives of the test?
   (iii) Does the test or tool appear to measure the subject matter (*e.g.,* congruency of triangles) or concept (*e.g.,* attitudes towards family planning) under consideration?

Content Validity

Content validity of a test is also established by adopting similar subjective approach as we do in the case of establishing face validity. However, its concept is wide and refers to more than just judging the validity of a test simply on the basis of its physical appearance of face value. Here a thorough examination and inspection of the contents of a test in reference to the objectives of the test forms the basis of the establishment of the needed validity. As a result, while establishing the content validity of his developed test, the test developer is required to make the value judgement on the appropriateness of its contents. For this purpose, items of the test are well screened and scruitinized for their appropriateness in reference to the realization of the test objectives.

Procedure for Establishing the Content Validity

The test developers may follow the same footsteps as followed for the establishment of the face validity of a test. In this connection while referring the test items to the panel of judges to evaluate them for establishing the validity of the test, they are requested to keep the following things and issues in mind:

1. Do the items included in the test cover the full range of the objectives of the test (*i.e.,* the concept to be measured, the behaviour to be assessed, and achievement or performance to be evaluated)?
2. To what extent the items of the test are representing the concept or behaviour they are supposed to measure (*i.e.,* appropriateness of the content of the test)?
3. Does the test or research tool adequately measure the major dimensions of the concept or behaviour under consideration through the items and scales used in the test?
4. Is the language used in writing the test items free from any ambiguity and inappropriateness? Is it capable to communicate what is needed for getting response from the respondents?

Criterion Related Validity

Unlike the face and content validities that are based on the logical subjectivity for the establishment of the reliability of a test or tool, the criterion related validity is based on empirical approach, *i.e.,* making planned comparisons to see if the developed instrument yields scores that relate to a criterion (Patten, 2007: 65).

What is the criterion? By a criterion used in the establishment of the validity of a test, we generally mean a standard against which a test or a test score is evaluated. This standard may be some already existing achievement test concurrently available for testing the same concept/contents as being measured by the test whose validity we want to establish. Since, here the test developer takes the help of a trusted external criterion currently available for establishing validity of his test, this type of validity is also named as concurrent validity. This type of validity for a test may be properly established by comparing the scores obtained on the developed test with the scores available on the currently available another trusted and valid tool (used for measuring the same concepts or contents of a particular subjects). Cohen and Swerdlik (2005: 164) have explained this process through a well meaning description given below:

> "*The concurrent validity* (*criterion related validity*) *of a particular test* (*Let's call it Test A*) *is explored with respect to another test* (*say Test B*). *In such studies, prior research has satisfactorily demonstrated the validity of Test B, and the question becomes 'How Well does Test A compare with Test B?' Here, Test B is used as the validating criterion.*"

Procedure for Establishing Criterion Related or Concurrent Validity

1. Administer the developed test on a representative sample of the population for which test has been developed and tabulate the scores (designated as scores 'X').
2. Administer the already standardized currently available achievement test (measuring the same concepts, contents and subject material related to a particular class or grade) on the same sample of the students and tabulate the scores (designated as scores 'Y).
3. Now compute Pearson product moment correlation between these two sets of scores 'X' and 'Y'.
4. In case the correlation coefficient so computed is significant, then get assured about the validity of your developed test.

Tools of Evaluation — Qualitative and Quantitative

What are Qualitative and Quantitative Evaluation Tools?

In evaluating the learning outcomes of the students a teacher has to make use of a number of tools and techniques helpful in collecting quantitative as well as qualitative data/information of varying nature. Depending upon the nature of information/data obtained through a measure of evaluation tools such as quantitative or qualitative, the tools and techniques are also respectively named as quantitative evaluation tools or qualitative tools. In this way, quantitative or qualitative evaluation tools are those assignment devices, techniques or tools that help in obtaining quantitative or qualitative data for explaining the type of quantitative or qualitative changes occurring in the behaviour of the learners through the specified learning experiences in one or the other learning situations. In other words quantitative evaluation tools help in quantitative measurement or description of the learning outcomes of the students. The scores derived from the use of achievement tests provide quantitative data and we can express the outcomes of these tests in terms of percentages, grades, division, etc. for the inter-individual comparisons *i.e.,* where does one stand in his class/school in terms of the scores earned in the test in comparison to his/her peers.

The major shortcoming or limitation with the use of quantitative tools (such as achievements) lies in their inability or incapacity to yield qualitative data or information, about the learning outcomes of the students. This deficit and limitation can be overcome with the use of one or the other qualitative tools. The measures of qualitative tools provide the necessary qualitative description of the performance level of the students demonstrating by them through different practical task and activities, constructive and creative output. Similar is the case with behavioural assessment. How far one has been able to bring needed changes in his behaviour, what is lacking or seems to be appreciable and encouraging in one's behaviour can only be properly revealed to him through qualitative description of the good and poor things observed or diagnosed in his behaviour through the help of qualitative tools. How one can improve his handwriting, oral communication, skills related to one or the other areas of knowledge and application, social and emotional behaviour, bring suitable modification in his attitudes, habits, ways of thinking and doing the things may be well supported through the detailed and analytic feedback provided by the measures taken through the qualitative evaluation tools.

Quantitative Evaluation Tools — Types and Description

The most commonly used quantitative tools for the assessment of the learning outcomes of the students in one or the other subjects of the school curriculum are concerned with the use of different types of achievement tests — Teacher made or standardized. A teacher may make use of them for the day to day assessment of the learning progress of the students or may make their use in the form of weekly, periodically, monthly, quarterly, half-yearly or yearly tests or examinations. These may be conducted in oral, written or practical mode under the name of oral/viva-voce examination, written examination and practical examination. Data derived from these tests/examinations in the form of numerical scores then can be subjected to quantitative data analysis for providing percentages, averages, percentiles leading to their generalizations in the form of grading and divisions.

In this way, quantitative evaluation tools used for the evaluation or assessment of the learning outcomes of the students may be mainly classified and categorized as under:

A. Oral tools and examinations
B. Practical tests and examination
C. Written tests and examination consisting of essay, short answer, very short answer and objective type questions.

Let us have necessary discussion over the nature and use of these commonly employed quantitative evaluation tools.

A. Oral Tests and Examination

These tools or examinations are based on oral communication between the examiner and examinees. Here in general oral questions, are put to the students for being responded by them in oral form. Besides question-answer, other verbal communication and dialogue techniques such as interviews, quizzes, group discussion, panel discussion, debets and declaration contests etc. may also be used for evaluating students' abilities and learning potential in oral form in all the three domain cognitive. Conative and affective of the behavioural outcomes.

B. Practical Tests or Examinations

In such tests or examination students are required and demonstrate their learning performances by engaging themselves in experimental and work activities. They have to create or produce something, report their observations of a relevant phenomenon, demonstrate the applicability of theoretical information in a concrete form and perform some motor behaviour or skilled activity as asked to be done for testing or evaluating their behavioural out comes related to the cognitive, conative and affective domains.

C. Written Tests or Examinations

These tests or examinations require writing material such as paper and pencil from the examiners and examinees. Students receive test questions in written mode, known as question paper and are required to give their responses on the supplied answer sheet or the question paper itself in the written form. The scoring and interpretation of these answer sheets or written responses thus becomes a basic for the evaluation of the teaching learning outcomes, performances and abilities of the students. Written test is the most frequently and popularly used evaluation technique.

The questions framed in these tests are usually of three types: (i) Essay, (ii) Short answer, and (iii) Objective. Let us know about all these three forms of test items.

Essay Type Questions in a written test (whether teacher made or standardised) are characterized with their demand from the students to respond by providing quite lengthy, descriptive, detailed and elaborate answers. The answers given by the students are so lengthy and descriptive that these might look like essays on the related subjects. Students are at liberty to respond to the presented questions in a way they like. The questions like following may be cited as illustrations for the setting of such essay type questions.

- Describe the possible cause responsible for the outcome of the Indian independence war of 1857.
- What are chemical and physical changes? Discuss with illustrations.
- How do we learn? Discuss in the light of the theories and principles of learning.

Short Answer Type Questions. Set in a written paper represent those questions which need a short and pinpointed reply either limited to fixed number of words say 100 or 200 words or restricted in its scope by delimitation and specification like list, define, give three examples, provide a most suitable reason, etc. For the illustration purpose we may cite the following questions.

- Define intelligence.
- Describe the role of rewards and punishment in maintaining class room discipline (write your answer in 100-150 words).
- Cite three examples each for distinguishing between physical and chemical changes.

Very Short Answer Type Questions. The responses or answers required for these question is quite short in nature. They may be as short as involving a word or two or one or two sentences at large. As illustration we are presenting a few very short answer type questions.

1. Name the capital and the chief minister of your state.
2. From where does river Ganga originate and end its journey?
3. Give one example each for physical and chemical changes.
4. What in Ohm's law?
5. Provide the formula for computing compound interest.
6. Name the three main winter crops of your region.
7. Tell the main distinction or identifying characteristic of hard and soft water.
8. Name the colours used in our National Flag.

Objective Type Questions. Set in a written form represent those type of questions which can be responded by just writing one or two words or numerals, filling up the blank or choosing one out of the multiple given responses, etc. The answer or answers to such questions are one and the same and are therefore do not vary from examinee to examinee. Their interpretation and scoring is also quite objective, reliable and valid. On account of requiring too less time for responding and writing the responses, a sufficient number of questions may be set in a given paper and this characteristic make them more comprehensive and useful for serving evaluation purpose in a more effective way. These objective type questions may appear in various forms in a written paper meant for the evaluation of the required achievements or performances. Below we cite some of the commonly used types.

1. True-False Type: This type of questions are in the form of a statement which may be either true or false. The student has to tell whether it is true or false by writing Yes/No. True/False, correct/incorrect or marking # or # at the given place.

Example: Below are given some statements you have to tell which one of them is true and which is false by encircling the true/false written in the right hand column. Don't encircle unless you are sure for its correctness or incorrectness because there will be negative marking for the incorrect responses.

	Statements	*Your Judgement*	
(i)	The sun rises in the west	True	False
(ii)	Sunlight is essential for the growth of plants.	True	False
(iii)	Mercury is a bad conductor of heat	True	False
(iv)	Sikkim is a Union Territory	True	False
(v)	The third battle of Panipat was fought in 1526.	True	False

2. Completion Type: In these type of questions students are asked to fill up the gaps left in the given statements by writing down suitable words or figures etc.

Example: Fill up the blanks:

(i) The instrument for measuring atmospheric pressure is known by the name ....

(ii) Days and nights are caused by .... motion of the earth.
(iii) The moon .... round the ....
(iv) 40°F is equal to .... degree centigrade.

3. Multiple Choice Type: In these type of questions a number of answers, say four or five, are given for each of the questions. Out of these answers only one is correct. The students are required to pick up the correct answer.

Example: Pick up the correct answer from the multiple choices given for a particular question and write it in the space given on the right hand side.

(i) The name of the instrument used for measuring temperature is:
(a) Barometer (b) Thermometer
(c) Hydrometer (d) Lactometer
(e) Voltmeter ( )

(ii) Air is heated by the sun through:
(a) Convection (b) Conduction
(c) Radiation (d) Convection and radiation
(e) Conduction and convection. ( )

(iii) Which state in India has a separate constitution?
(a) Sikkim (b) Goa
(c) Nagaland (d) Jammu and Kashmir ( )

4. Matching Type: These type of questions have two columns, one for the questions and the other for answers. The answers written in the second column are not necessarily of the same order as the questions in the first column. The students are required to match the answers with their respective questions. To put check on guessing, the number of answers given in the right hand column may be kept one more or less than the number of questions on the left hand side.

Example 1. Match the answers for Column B with the questions in the Column A and write the suitable number in the space provided.

Column A	*Column B*	
(a) Unit of measuring heat	(i) Watts	( )
(b) Unit of measuring wavelength	(ii) Calories	( )
(c) Unit of measuring electric resistance	(iii) Hertz	( )
(d) Unit of measuring power	(iv) Ohms	( )
(e) Unit of measuring temperature	(v) Degrees	( )

Example 2. Match the following items in the two columns:

Column A (*Nobel prize awarded*)	*Column B* (*Field*)	*Correct answer Code*
(i) R.N. Tagore	(a) Peace	( )
(ii) C.V. Raman	(b) Physics	( )
(iii) Mother Teresa	(c) Medicine	( )
(iv) Amartya Sen	(d) Literature	( )
(v) Hargovind Khurana	(e) Economics	( )

5. *Simple Recall Type:* In these questions, there are simple interrogative sentences which require very brief answers in the form of a single word or figure.

Example:

(i) Name the type of image formed by the plane mirror. ( )
(ii) Name the gas employed for disinfecting drinking water. ( )
(iii) Where is the largest goldmine in India? ( )
(iv) Which state is the largest producer of copper in India? ( )
(v) What is the chemical name of vinegar? ( )
(vi) Name the scientist who introduced the equation $E = mc^2$ ( )

6. *Time Sequence Type:* In such questions students are asked to provide sequential order for the given events/incidents/happenings, etc. Few examples are as follows.

(a) A few historical events are provided here. Arrange them in a proper sequence by numbering as 1, 2, 3, 4, 5, etc. according to their time sequence.

Kalinga victory of emperor Ashoka ( )
Invasion of India by Alexander ( )
The separation of Bangladesh from Pakistan ( )
The battle of Haldi Ghati ( )
The battle of Plassey ( )
The establishment of East India Company ( )

(b) Arrange the following events related to First War of Independence, 1857 in a proper time sequence

Emergence of Lord Canning as Governor General ( )
Emergence of Lord Dalhousie as Governor General ( )
Curtailing of the pension to Nana Sahib ( )
Denial of the permission to adopt a child as son to Laxmi Bai ( )
Ordering the Mughal emperor to leave the fort and palace ( )
Hanging of Mangal Pandey ( )

7. *Discriminating or 'odd man out' type questions:* In these types of questions, there are a few names of things, persons or events except those ones which may be grouped together on account of some type of similarity among them. The students are asked to single out the one which does not go along with others. Some examples are as follows:

(i) Akbar, Jahangir, Bahadurshah, Muhammad Shah, Dara Sikoh, Shuja, Balban ( )
(ii) Tantya Tope, Bahadur Shah Jaffar, Kanwar Singh, Nana Sahib, Laxmi Bai, Subhash Chandra Base ( )
(iii) Hyderabad, Mumbai, Shimla, Chandigarh, Bhopal, Sikandrabad, Trivendrum ( )

Planning and Preparation of an Achievement Test (Including Blue Print)

The teachers in the classroom face the need of constructing or developing a teacher made test for the assessment of the learning outcomes of their students in one or the other teaching subjects. For this purpose they must be well acquainted with the procedure and the needed essentials for the construction of an appropriate achievement test such as nature of the items/questions of the test — their selection, organization and providing it a final form for its administration and interpretation. In this chapter, we would like to throw light on these essentials related to the construction/development of an achievement test.

A. Construction/Selection of the Test Items

What type of items/questions should be there in an achievement test, the consideration about it, occupies a key place in the construction or development of an achievement test. The things like below as guidelines may prove helpful in selecting/constructing the items of the test.

1. *Keep in view the objectives of assessment:* A test is constructed or developed for the assessment of the learning outcomes of the students in one or the other learning or subject area. What type of learning outcomes or performances are to be assessed should be quite clear for the test developer. For this purpose he should try to lay down first the objectives of the test and define them in terms of specific behaviour changes expected in the students as the result of studying a particular unit or course of study for the assessment of which the test is being developed.

2. *Keep in view the coverage of the syllabus or contents:* The contents which have to be covered in the test are directly dependent upon what has been taught by the teacher. The teacher should keep an outline of the learning experiences given by him. Although no major unit or subtopic of what has been taught should be left, yet it is not essential at all to ask for each and every thing discussed by the teacher in the class. In other words a reasonable coverage of various aspects of the learning experiences given to the students should be the goal.

3. *Decide about the types of items or questions*: Decision about the types of questions to be set in the test paper is also an essential aspect of its construction. All the three forms — essay type, short answer type and objective type should find place in a good achievement test,

4. *Keep in view the time allotted for the administration of the test*: The selection/construction of the test items are also dependent upon the time duration fixed for the administration of the test. It should be lengthy or short depending upon the time available for its administration. On the other hand, if assessment objectives need so the length and duration of the test may be arranged accordingly.

B. Preparation of the Blue Print

This is the most crucial step in the planning of the test. Blue-print is a sort of the design for the test paper in which we present a detailed questions wise distribution of marks over specific objectives, topics and forms of questions. Therefore, all the factors mentioned in the above four steps *i.e.*, objectives to be tested, contents to be covered, types of questions to be asked and total time to be given, should be kept in mind while preparing the blue print or design of the test.

How the blue print is prepared can be understood through the following illustration:

BLUE PRINT

Objectives	*Knowledge*			*Understanding*			*Application*			*Total*
Format of the question →	E	S	O	E	S	O	E	S	O	
Sub Unit ↓										
Digestive System	2	2	1	–	1	2	–	1	1	10
	(1)	(2)	(1)		(1)	(2)		(1)	(1)	
Blood Circulatory System	2	2	1	–	1	2	–	1	1	10
	(1)	(2)	(1)		(1)	(2)		(1)	(1)	
Respiratory System	–	1	1	–	1	1	–	–	1	5
		(1)	(1)		(1)	(1)			(1)	
Sub Total	4	5	3	–	3	5	–	2	3	25
	(2)	(5)	(3)		(3)	(5)		(2)	(3)	
Total		**12**			**8**			**5**		

Note: Digits Given in The brackets indicate the number of questions set and out side the brackets provide the marks associated with the questions.

SUMMARY

Question Type	*Number of questions*	*Marks*	*Other Descriptions*
Essay Type	2	4	(i) Scheme of option-None
S-short Answer Type	10	10	(ii) Scheme of Sections
O-objective Type	11	11	–Part (A) Essay Type
Total	23	25	–Part (B) Short Answer Type
			–Part (C) Objective Type

C. Organising and Arranging the Items or Questions

The items or questions to be included in the test require proper organization and arrangement. The following points may prove helpful in this direction.

(i) Essay and objective items should be kept in two separate sections with separate time limit for each. Short answer questions can be tagged on the either of these two sections according to their nature.

(ii) Each section should also have separate instructions in addition to the instruction common to both the sections,

(iii) Items should be arranged in order of difficulty from the easy to the more difficult,

(iv) In objective type of items it is advisable not to use too many different forms of items or questions as it involves some waste of time over reading instructions, etc. As far as possible multiple choice items should be preferred as they are more reliable, valid and objective in comparison to other forms of items.

(v) It is better to have 20 to 30% items in excess so that in final review after items analysis the excess item may left out.

D. Try out and Item Analysis

After doing as suggested above the test so prepared must be administered to an appropriate sample of students for its try out and suggested task of item analysis. Item analysis is mainly carried out, serving the following useful functions:

- For finding out non-clarity, ambiguities, mistakes etc.
- For determining difficulty value of each item.
- For determining discriminating value of each item.

With the help of such analysis we can modify or get rid of defective items carrying ambiguities, mistakes and non-clarity as well as having too low discriminating and too high difficulty values.

How to Carryout Item Analysis

Both qualitative and quantitative item analysis needs to be performed for getting rid of the incompetent items. Let us discuss the processes of carrying out these item analysis.

Qualitative Item Analysis

Here the items of the test are subjected to close scrutiny on the part of the test developer. He may also seek the opinion of some experienced teachers and experts for deriving conclusion about.

(i) Which items of the test are not comprehensible or ambiguous and why?

(ii) Are the instructions given in the test clear and suitable for item responses? If not, how the necessary improvement can be made?

(iii) Are the items helpful in assessing of what they sought to assess? If not, point out the items failing in this mission.

(iv) Is there any mistake in the language used or numericals provided in the test? Suggest the correction.

With the feedback received on the above account, the necessary correction and replacement must be made in the test items.

Quantitative Item Analysis

The task of Quantitative item analysis involves computation of discriminating and difficulty values of each item. Let us know about the method of computing these values.

(i) Computation of discriminating value or index: Measure of item discrimination indicate how adequately an item separates or discriminates between high scores and low scores on an entire test. In other words, it is concerned with seeing how far a particular item is capable of discriminating between the good achievers and poor achievers on the test. For assessing such ability of an item related to its discriminating power, a statistical value known as item discrimination index is required to be computed by the test developer.

$$\text{Index of item discrimination} = \frac{A-B}{N/2}$$

Where A = the number of correct scores from the high scoring group (say top 25 or 33 per cent)

B = the number of correct scores from the low scoring group (say bottom 25 or 33 per cent)

N = the total number of students in the two groups

Let us illustrate the use of the above formula with an example.

A test developer tried to test the first draft of his achievement test on a representative sample of 60 students. It was a multiple choice test. Each correct response here was marked as 1. On the basis of the total scores earned by them on the entire test, he divided them into three groups — high scoring group, average scoring group and low scoring group (each sub-groups consisting of 20 students). He computed the values of A and B, *i.e.,* the number of correct scores on a particular item from the high and low scoring group.

On the first item of the test, he found that:

(i) there were 16 students who responded correctly to item no. 1 from the high scoring group of 20 students, and

(ii) there was only one student from the lower group of 20 students who was able to respond correctly to this item.

In this way, after arriving at the value of A as 16 and value of B as 1, he put these values in the formula for computing the index of item discrimination for the item no. 1 in the following way:

Index of item discrimination = (16 – 1) /1/2 (20 + 20) = 15 /20 = 0.75

It is to be noted that the maximum value for the indiscrimination index of an item of the test is 1.00. We also know that it is customary to make use of the value 0.67 of the indiscrimination index as the critical value for retaining or excluding an item from the test (however, it is not a compulsion). However, in our case the value of indiscriminative index for item no. 1 is 0.75. It is higher than the critical value of 0.67. Hence, it can be safely concluded that the item no. 1 is capable of discriminating between the high and low achievers on the test.

And therefore it is to be retained in the test.

(ii) Computation of difficulty value or Index: Item difficulty of an item refers to its difficulty level, *i.e.,* how much difficult or easy it is for replying to it on the part of the group of students who are appearing in the test. For assessing the difficulty level of an item, a statistical value, known as item difficulty index, is required to be computed by the test developer.

The formula used for computing this index for each item runs as below:

$$\text{Index of item difficulty} = A/N \times 100$$

Where A = the number of students who answered the item correctly

N = the total number of students who attempted the item

The maximum value for the index of item difficulty like index of item discrimination is also 1.00. The cut-off or critical index value for terming a particular item as difficult is 0.67 and as easy is 0.33. Therefore, the items falling below 33 per cent and above 67 per cent may be termed too difficult and too easy, respectively. Here, it should again be noted that there is no compulsion for the test developer to reject an item with an index of difficulty below or above the cut-off points. If he feels the need of retaining this item in spite of it being too difficult or easy level, he can do so. Moreover, the decision about using a particular value of index as a critical or cut-off point also varies from situation to situation. For example, in the case of norm-referenced testing the item difficulty should be around 50 per cent.

E. Designing or preparing the final form of the test

As a result of try out and item analysis of the test the improper items can be deleted from the test. In addition few items may be suitably modified or even added for making the test more functionable. This final form should then be got printed/photostated/cyclostyled as the situation demands for the needed evaluation of the students achievements.

F. Developing Guidelines for Administration and Scoring

A test developer should try to specify and issue guidelines for the administration and scoring of the test. He should provide specific instructions for the administration of the test, by mentioning the conditions needed for the administration of the test, the means and material that is specifically required for the administration of the test and precautions, if any for the administration of the test. Regarding scoring it is always advisable on the part of a test developer to provide a scoring key. It is not only the presence of objective type items that require an advance preparation of a scoring key but also in case of essay and short answer type questions, the answer and procedure for scoring should be pre-determined specifying the things like below:

(i) The division of marks according to the sections or subsections in which an essay type question has been distributed.

(ii) The number of steps or points expected in the answer.
(iii) The number of lines or words expected for covering the answers of short and very short answer type questions.
(iv) The weightage given to the steps or points expected in the answer of the students.
(v) The nature of the model answer and weightage given for the steps or points explanation, illustration, etc. mentioned in the model answer.
(vi) Weightage given to the diagram, sketches, tables and illustration etc.

By following the steps narrated above, teachers can manage to develop the needed teacher made achievement tests for evaluating the progress of the students at the end of the delivery of their lesson or covering up of a specific unit or course during a session.

Qualitative Evaluative Tools: Types and Description

In the assessment of learning or behavioural outcomes of the students, there arise a number of occasions where we desperately need the information or data in the form of qualitative description in place of the quantitative description such as numerical scores, marks or grading. These may involve the situation where we want to give the learner's feedback in qualitative descriptive form about their performance in some activities, the strength and weaknesses related to their creation and product or the behavioural performance demonstrated by them as a result of some behavioural improvement/modification, progress etc. In these situations, we have to take the help of one or the other qualitative assessment device or tool. The commonly employed qualitative assessment tools in this concern may be named as below.

1. Observation
2. Introspection
3. Projection
4. Sociometry
5. Interview
6. Rating scales
7. Check lists
8. Use of performance based activities
9. Use of seminar, Symponum, Panel discussion, etc.

However, here, we would be focusing our discussion on the first four of the above mentioned qualitative evaluation tools.

Let us discuss them now one by one.

Observation as a Tool for Qualitative Assessment

Observation can be employed as an effective device or tool for collecting information or data in a qualitative descriptive form about the quality of one's performance including the changes brought out in the affective behaviour domain. Let us see what we mean by the term observation as an evaluation device and how it can be made into use for collecting qualitative data.

What is Observation?

Observation refers to a process of observing a thing, person, phenomenon or event with the use of one's sensory organs for knowing something related to its nature and ways of behaving or occurrence. We can make use of our all the five senses—Sense of vision, hearing, touch, smell and taste for carrying out the task of observation on our part. However, in general, the two senses — Senses of vision and hearing are more commonly used in assessing the outcomes of the changes brought out in conative and affective behaviour of the students through the way and means of formal and informal education. We can watch and hear the things related to the performance of the students in various activities representing the changes introduced in conative and affective domain of their behaviour.

The Styles and Ways of Observation

Observation as a tool is employed in assessing the behavioural aspects of the subjects in a number of ways and styles classified in the manner given below:

A. On the basis of the very nature of observation or formalities observed in observing.
(i) Formal observation (ii) Informal observation.

B. On the basis of the structural framework of the phenomena of observation involved in observation.
(i) Structured observation (ii) Unstructured observation.

C. On the basis of the degree of involvement of the observer.
(i) Participant observation (ii) Non-participant observation.

Let us discuss these various types of observation in relation to the collection of information or data.

1. Formal observation: In such a type or style of observation, it is carried out in quite a formal way by observing the necessary formalities like (i) providing the information to the individual or individuals about the nature and purpose of the observation (ii) the date, timings and place of observation (iii) the names and introduction of the observers (*iv*) the necessary pre-preparation needed on the part of the subjects for such an observation just as showing of any maintained record or preparing them or their environment for such inspection etc. However, such a type of observation cannot prove more fruitful in terms of drawing some reliable and valid conclusions about one's behaviour or personality. For example, if we announce to the inmates of a hostel that we are going to have an inspection of their rooms regarding their habit of cleanliness on a particular date and time, such type of a formally announced observation will surely fail in its objective of knowing about the habit of cleanliness among the hostlers. The prior information, will automatically make them quite alert.

Thus, the cleanliness behaviour shown at the time of such formal observation will not be a true representation of their real behaviour. It will have an artificial mask with the aim of turning the results of the observation in their favour. Hence the reliability and validity of the collected information can remain in doubt for collecting data through the method of formal observation.

2. *Informal observation:* Contrary to the formal observation, informal observation is carried out in a quite informal, spontaneous and natural way. Here no prior information about the nature, purpose, timings and place of the observation is given to the individual or individuals. They are thus caught unaware, engaging in their behavioural activities in a quite usual and natural way. In such naturalistic observational situations we may have a relatively true picture of the behavioural characteristics and the state of things and events lying in one's environment.

3. *Structured observation:* As the name suggests, the observation process carried out in this type of observation is quite structured, fixed and pre-determined irrespective of the fact that it is organised in a formal or non-formal way. Processing of such observation essentially requires proper structuring and standardization of the conditions of observation by specifying (i) the things or events to be observed, (ii) data to be recorded (iii) the assisting tools *e.g.* checklists and rating scales to be employed (iv) the recording devices like tape recorder, video makers, telescope, etc. are used.

4. *Unstructured observation:* The observation process adopted in such observation is totally unstructured *i.e.* no conditions or restrictions are imposed upon the observer in carrying out observation for the collection of information or data. The purpose of such unstructured observation is to provide a richer and more true spontaneous account of the things and events happening in one's environment with a lot of freedom and flexibility in his hand. It does not make use of the structured material/devices like checklist rating scales etc. for the observations of pre-determined things or events.

5. *Participant observation:* This type of observation requires on the part of the evaluator to play the role of a participant observer while observing a thing, event or phenomena in a particular observing situation. In observation actually the role of the observer may be placed on a continuum ranging from the complete participant to the complete non-participant *i.e.* complete participation to complete detachment as a mere observer. The role of the complete observer according to Gold (1958) is typified in the one-way mirror, the video cassette, the audio-cassette and the photograph, whilist complete participation involves researchers taking on membership roles (overt or covert) declaring or non-declaring his identity as the observer.

In this way, participant observation may be defined as a type of observation in which the observer takes the membership role of the group to be observed by declaring or not declaring his identity as an observer to the group. By joining the group thus he may share the observed situations as a visiting stranger, an attentive listener, an eager learner, or as a complete participant overt observer (registering recording and interpreting behaviour of the group). The participant observer, thus may found to play a double role. On one hand he acts and feels like other members of the group by being engaged in the group activities and on the other hand works as an observer to note down the things related to the behaviour of the members and events occurring in the group situations. For example, a teacher while assessing students may join them in the laboratory or workshop activities or accompany them on tour and excursion activities for having a close observation of them. Such a type of observation may provide good opportunity for the observation of the behaviour of the individuals. However, it suffers from a serious limitation as the presence of an observer may obstruct the natural and spontaneous flow of the behaviour activities of those individuals.

6. Non-participant observation: This type of observation tries to do away with the above cited defect or limitation of the participant observation. Here the observer observes the behaviour of the individuals in such a way that they may not have any idea about the observation of their behaviour in any way by one or the other observer. For this purpose as observer he may take his position on such a place in such a way, that while the individuals under observation may not see him but he can clearly watch and hear if possible all about their behaviour in action. There may be a screen or a curtain of such a nature as to help an observer in real observation while hiding his presence.

The use of some modern equipments like secret cameras, video recording, audio recording, etc. may also serve such purposes. While sitting at quite a far distance, he may also take the help of a telescope for a clear secret observation. Whatever means and methods may be employed by the observer, his motive in such an observation always remains to come into contact with the natural and spontaneous behaviour of the subject without making him aware of his presence.

Utilizing Observation Tool for Assessing Behavioural Outcomes

The use of the observation tool for the task of assessing behavioural outcomes involves the two systematic phases.

Phase I. Planning and Preparation for Observation

The success of an observation depends much on its proper planning and preparation. This initial task requires proper attention on the following aspects —

- What type of behavioural activities situations or events are to be assessed through observation?

- How the observation work is to be carried out, what type of methods or resources will be used for such observation?
- What type of situation or environment is to be maintained for carrying out effective observation?
- How can the observation results may be made more reliable informative, objective and valid?

Phase II. Execution of the Observations Task

This second step is related with the actual observation work done by the observer as per planning and pre-preparation made in the first step. Here as far as possible the best methods and techniques should be used for the observation of the behaviour depending upon the purpose of observation and availability of the resources and environmental situations at the time of observation. In this concern for obtaining better results, the following things should always be kept in mind—

- The subject should not have any idea that his behaviour is under observation. As far as possible his behaviour is to be observed in a quite naturalistic condition for deriving the sample of his most natural and spontaneous behaviour.
- The observation work must be carried out properly in a quite effective way. The eyes have to play a key role in such an observation. If possible, one should also try to hear about the behavioural activities in action.
- It is always better to make use of a telescope for viewing the activities of individuals specially while sitting at a far off place.
- There must be an adequate arrangement for using the modern observation equipments like cameras, video and audio recording. The use of these appliances not only helps in proper observation of the behavioural activities but proves an automatic recording device for the proper analysis and interpretation of the behaviour.
- It is not proper to rely over the results of a single observation for informing about the nature of the things, events or behaviour observed. For a desirable objectivity, reliability and validity, such observation work must be repeated by the same observer for a desirable number of times or it should be carried out by a number of different observers at one or a number of times.
- The recording about the nature of a thing, event or trait of a person should always be done side by side by the observer during the process of observation. The failure to do so prove quite costly as the observer may forget or miss some or the other important things or links regarding the observed phenomenon.

The observer may do it effectively with the help of noting down the things in short or in a symbolic way easily understood by him later on. He may also take the help of a checklist, and/or rating scale for tallying or marking the things to be observed in the observed phenomenon. However, in case he has to play the role of a participant observer, then the recording of the observed phenomenon may be proceeded in the manner below suggested by Loftland (1971).

- Make careful mental notes of all that is observed.
- Note down important events, words or quotes which are susceptible to memory lapses.
- As soon as possible, prepare full field notes by converting mental and jotted down notes into meaningful observational notes.

Introspection as a Tool for Qualitative Assessment

It is the oldest tool or technique known for the study of behaviour. In the earlier days of the studies carried out in the areas of philosophy, sociology and psychology, the behaviour was studied only through a kind of self-examination or inner observation called introspection. Let us try to look into the meaning of the word introspection in order to understand this method.

Introspection is composed of two words — "intro" and "spection". Intro means 'within or inward' and spection means 'looking'. Hence introspection means looking within or looking inward. It is inner perception. Therefore, in introspection, one is required to get inside one's own mind. It is a sort of self-observation in which one perceives, analyses and reports one's own feelings and, in fact, everything that takes place in one's mind during the course of a mental act. For example, when in the state of anxiety, fear or anger, one may be asked to discover by one's own observation what he sensed, thought or felt at the time of experiencing that sort of emotion.

Merits of Introspection Method

Introspection — the self-observation and reporting of one's own mental processes possesses some unique advantages as mentioned below.

1. It is a simple and readily available method. Our mental processes are always with us and can be introspected at any moment. Thereby, introspection is able to give us a direct and immediate knowledge of our own mental processes without involving any extra expenditure for the material or apparatus.

2. Moreover, introspection provides us with an adequate knowledge of the inner or covert experiences. Thus, the inner behaviour of an individual in the form of thinking or feeling something can be revealed through introspection

Demerits and Limitations of Introspection Method

However, introspection, as a method of studying behaviour, suffers from some serious drawbacks and limitations such as:

1. In introspection, one needs to observe or examine carefully one's mental processes in the form of thoughts, feelings or sensations. The state of our mental process is continuously changing. Therefore when we

concentrate to introspect a particular phase of our mental activity that phase passes off. For example, when we get angry with a person and afterwards sit down calmly to introspect or self-examine, the state of anger is sure to be passed on. So what one tries to observe is not what is happening at that time with oneself but what has happened some time before.

2. Introspection as a method of study seriously lacks reliability, validity and objectivity on the following grounds:

(i) The results lack in reliable communicability and repeatability. Here, one investigator can never be sure that what he feels or senses is the same as what other investigators do. For example, if we invite the introspection reports on the nature of the sensation of "green", these reports are bound to differ. Some will insist that green is a unitary sensation, where others will say that green is a mixed sensation involving yellow and blue. We have no arrangement for the objective observation of the introspection phenomenon. Moreover, in introspection, one studies one's own behaviour or mental process. It is not possible to verify the individual's self-observation as there is no provision for studying one's mind by others in introspection.

(ii) It is next to impossible to acquire validity and exactness in self-observation or examination of one's mental process. The mind in perceiving its own functions tries to divide itself into two halves — the subject and the object. The object of observation and the instrument of observation are just one and the same. It automatically affects the validity and exactness of the observational process and the derived results. A man who is angry or afraid cannot exactly observe what is going on in his mind and remains unchanged in his emotional state of anger or fear. The consciousness on his part is sure to affect his mental or emotional state which is the object of observation.

3. Introspection as a method of studying behaviour has a very limited scope. It can only be applied satisfactorily in case of adult normal human beings. The behaviour of children, abnormal human beings, animals, etc. cannot be studied by this method.

In this way, if we try to evaluate the introspection method we would find that this method is based on self-speculation, lacks reliable communicability, repeatability and reasonable exactness or certainty. It is neither sufficiently scientific nor so practicable or simple to handle. Therefore, it cannot be taken as an adequate or sufficient single method for psychological studies. The conclusions arrived at by this method need to be supported on specific scientific grounds by taking the help of some other objective and reliable method.

Projective Techniques as a Tool for Qualitative Evaluation

Most of the tools and techniques utilized for the evaluation of the learning or behavioural outcomes of the students are those techniques which usualy assess or evaluate the overt or conscious behaviour of an individual. The covert or unconscious behaviour, by all means, is not so insignificant, rather it is more significant than the former, as Freud believes that our conscious behaviour is only one-tenth of the total behaviour. Therefore, there should be some other techniques which not only emphasize on the observable part of the human personality but can reveal his inner or private world and go deeper in the unconscious behaviour of an individual to dig out the repressed feelings, wishes, desires, fear, hopes and ambitions, etc.

Projective techniques are devised to accept the challenge. They try to assess the total personality of an individual and not in fragments. Let us see what these techniques are.

What are the Projective Techniques?

These techniques are based on the phenomenon of projection. In these techniques relatively indefinite and unstructured stimuli (like vague pictures, ink-blots, incomplete sentences, etc.) are provided to the subject and he is asked to structure them in any way he likes. In doing so he unconsciously projects his own desires, hope, fears, repressed wishes, etc. and thus not only reveals his inner or private world but gives a proper clue to estimate his total personality.

The common Projective Techniques are:

THE RORSCHACH INK-BLOT TEST

This technique has been developed by the Swiss psychologist, Mr. Harmans Rorschach. Material of the test consists of 10-cards on which we have ink-blots. Five of them are in black and white and five are multi-coloured. These ink-blots are completely unstructured — the shapes of the blots do not have any specific meaning.

Fig. 3.1: An ink-blot similar to that used in Rorschach test

Administration of the Test:

(i) The cards are presented one at a time in a specific order. When the subject takes his seat, the examiner gives him the first card with necessary instructions. He is asked to say what he sees in it, what does it look like, etc.

(ii) The subject is allowed as much time as he wants for a given card and is permitted to give as many responses to it as he wishes. He is also allowed to turn the card around and look at it from any angle to find things in it.

(iii) Besides keeping a record of the responses of the subject concerning these ink-blots on different pieces of paper, the examiner notes the time taken for each response, position in which cards are being held, emotional expression and other incidental behaviour of the subject during the test period etc.

(iv) After all the cards have been presented, the second phase of inquiry follows. It is intended to seek clarification or addition to original responses.

Scoring, Analysis and Interpretation of the Test: For the purpose of scoring, the responses are given specific symbols which are entered in 4 columns.

These scoring categories are named as:

(i) Location, (ii) Contents, (*iii*) Originality, and (*iv*) Determinants.

Location (*The first column*): Location refers to the part of the blot with which the subject associates each response. The symbol W.D.d and s are used for scoring the location responses. The symbols stand for the things given ahead:

- W for that response which shows that the subject is seeing the card as a whole.
- D indicate large details.
- d indicates small details.
- s indicates the subject's response to the white spaces within the main outlines.

Contents (*2nd column*). This column concerns itself with the contents of the responses. It simply takes note of what is seen by the subject and not the manner of its perception. Below we write some of the symbols used for scoring the content of the responses:

Scoring symbol.	*Content of the response*
H	Subject sees human forms
A	Subject sees animal forms
A_d or H_d	Subject sees animal detail or human detail
N	Subject sees natural objects like rivers mountains, green fields etc.
O	Subject sees inanimate objects like lamp shade, pot, etc.

In this way, for details of the contents the symbols are used and entered into the 2nd column.

Originality (*3rd column*): For each of 10 cards, certain responses are scored as popular, by symbol P, because of their common occurrence while some others in which something new is given, and thus indicates some type of originality in them, are scored as original depicted by the symbol O.

Determinants (*4th column*): This column takes note of the manner of perception, *i.e.* the particular characteristics which have helped the subject in determining the blot or deciding his manner of perception. The main determinants are:

(i) the form (F) of the blot, (ii) its colour (C),
(iii) movement (M), and (iv) shading (K).

For example, if the subject responds to a blot as butterfly, then, we can say that it is the "form" which led to this way of seeing it and then we score the response as F. On the other hand, if the subject sees something like fire, blood, etc. then the determinant is certainly the "colour" and we enter C in the fourth column.

Subject's responses on account of "shading", *e.g.* perception of rough or smooth surfaces, smoke, cloud etc., are scored as K, whereas if the subject responds in terms of "movements" — movement of human beings (like boy running, dancing, etc.), animal being (like dog barking) or inanimate objects (water flowing, cloth moving, etc.), the symbols, M, f_m or m are entered in the 4th column of determinants. We can have cases where we note them by mixed symbols as (CF), (FK), etc.

Interpretation. Now, in all the four columns the different symbols are counted. It gives an idea of the relative frequencies of different kinds of responses. The entry of scores (in symbols) in different columns can be roughly made in the following way:

	I Column Location					*II Column Contents*						*III Column Originally*		*IV Column Determinants*				+
Symbols	W	D	d			H	A	Ad	Hd	N	O	P	O	P	C	K	M	Mixed Category
Frequency																		

The relative frequencies of the different symbols within the scoring categories and among the several categories help the interpreter to decide the personality characteristics of the subject. For example, if

(i) the number of W's are greater than d or D; then the person is said to be mature, intelligent and is expected to possess the ability to synthesize.
(ii) More frequency on the side of the colour at the expense of human movement indicates an extrovert nature while domination of M over colour, an introvert.
(iii) Dominance of shading responses expresses anxiety, depressed attitudes and feeling of inferiority, and
(iv) Relatively more emphasis on movement indicates richness of one's imaginative life.

It is not only the relative importance or occurrence of certain kinds of responses which help in interpretation, the various other factors like time factor, the behaviour of the subject at the time of reactions etc. also have their meanings.

Therefore, it is only through various kinds of relationships, observations, records and integration of results from various parts that a final global picture about a subject's personality can be drawn. The test demands a lot of training and skill in scoring and interpretation on the part of the examiner and therefore, the work should be considered as a serious one and should only be done by an experienced and trained psychologist.

TAT OR THEMATIC APPRECIATION TEST

The test consisting of perception of a certain picture in a thematic manner (revealing imaginative themes) is called TAT or Thematic Appreciation Test. This test was developed by Murray and Morgan.

Fig. 3.2: A Sample Picture from **TAT**

Test material and administration: It consists of 30 pictures which portray human beings in *a* variety of actual life situations. Ten of the cards are meant for males, 10 for females and 10 for both. In this way, the maximum number of pictures used with any subject is 20. The test is usually; administered in two sessions, using 10 pictures in each session.

The pictures are presented one at a time. They are vague and indefinite. The subject is told clearly that this is a test of creative imagination and that there is no right and wrong response. He has to make up a story for each of the pictures presented to him, within a fixed time. He has to take care of the following aspects while knitting the story:

(i) What is going on the picture?
(ii) What has led to this scene?
(iii) What would happen in such a situation?

In making up the stories the subject unconsciously projects so many characteristics of his personality. There is no time to think. Therefore, the stories express his own life natural desires, likes and dislikes, ambitions, emotions, sentiments, etc. Its special value resides in its power of exploring the underlying hidden dries, complexes and conflicts of the personality. An expert examiner can know much about the personality of his subject by carefully interpreting the given responses.

Scoring and Interpretation: Originally Murray analyzed the contents of the stories according to need and presses (the need of the hero and the environmental forces to which he is exposed). Today this way of interpretation is not generally followed. Now a days, the system of scoring and interpretation takes account of the following:

(i) *Hero of the story.* What type of personality he has?

(ii) *Theme of the story.* What is the nature of the theme or plot used in making the story?

(iii) *The style of the story.* Length of the story, language used, direct or indirect expression, forced or poor expression, organisation of the contents, originality and creativity, etc.

(iv) *The content of the story.* What interests, sentiments, attitudes they depict. In which manner (reality or fantasy) the behaviour has been expressed. What inner state of the mind, the story reveals.

(v) *Test situation as a whole.* The subject's reaction to be listed as a whole.

(vi) *Particular emphasis or omissions.* The omission, addition, distortion and attention to particular details.

(vii) *Subject's attitude, towards authority and sex.*

(viii) *Outcome, conclusion of the story,* happy, unhappy, comedy, etc.

As a whole, the recurring themes and features contribute more than a single response towards interpretation. Moreover, the global view of one's personality should be based on the responses of all the 20 pictures shown to the subject. There are so many chances of misinterpreting the stories contents by an immature examiner. Therefore, the future of TAT hangs on the possibility of perfecting the interpreter more than in perfecting the material. He should be given full opportunity for acquiring essential knowledge and training for this purpose.

CAT (CHILDREN APPERCEPTION TEST)

TAT test works well with adults and adolescents but for children it is not suitable. For children between 3 to 10 years, the CAT was developed by D. Leopold Bellak.

Description of the Test: It consists of 10 cards. The cards have pictures of animals instead of human characters since it was thought that children could identify themselves with animal figures more readily than with persons. These animals are shown in various life situations. For both sexes, all the 10 cards are needed. The pictures are designed to evoke fantasies relating to a child's own experience, reactions and feeling. Whatever story the child makes, he projects himself. It is a colour free test but it demands some alterations according to the child's local conditions.

Administering the Test: All the 10 cards are presented one by one and the subject is asked to make up stories on them. The child should have confidence and he should take story making a pleasant game to play with.

Interpretation: Interpretation of the stories is centred round the following eleven variables:

(i) *Hero.* The personality traits of the hero as revealed by the story.

(ii) *Theme of the Story.* What particular theme has he selected for the story building?

(iii) *The end of the story.* Happy ending or unhappy, wishful, realistic or unrealistic.

(iv) *Attitude towards parental figures.* Hatred, respectful, devoted, grateful, dependent, aggressive and fearful, etc.

(v) *Family role.* With whom in the family the child identifies himself.

(vi) *Other outside figures introduced.* Objects of the elements introduced in the story but not shown in the picture.

(vii) *Omitted or ignored figures.* Which figures are omitted or ignored should be noted as they may depict the wish of the subject that the figures were not there.

(viii) *Nature of the anxieties.* Harassment, loss of love, afraid of being left alone etc., should also be noted.

(ix) *Punishment for crime.* The relationship between a crime committed in the story and severity of punishment given for it.

(x) *Defence and confidence.* The type of defences, flight, aggression, passivity, regression, etc. the child takes, nature of compliance or dependence, involvement in pleasure and achievement, sex desire etc.

(xi) *Other supplementary knowledge.* The language, the overall structure of the stories, time taken for completing them and the reactions of the subject at the time of making the story etc..

With all this knowledge an expert interpreter can pronounce judgement on the various aspects of the child's personality.

WORD ASSOCIATION TEST

In this technique there are a number of selected words. The subject is told that:

(i) the examiner will utter a series of words, one at a time.

(ii) after each word the subject is to reply as quickly as possible with the first word that comes to his mind, and

(iii) there is no right or wrong response.

The examiner then records the reply to each word spoken by him; the reaction time and any unusual speech or behaviour manifestations accompanying a given response. The contents of the responses along with the other recorded things give clues for evaluating the human personality and thus help a psychologist in his work.

SENTENCE-COMPLETION TESTS

These tests include a list of incomplete sentences, generally open at the end, which require completion by the subject in one or more words. The subject is asked to go through the list and answer as quickly as possible (without giving a second thought to his answers). For example, we can have the following sentences:

I am worried over..........

My hope is..........

I feel proud when........

My hero is..........

The Sentence completion tests are regarded as superior to Word Association because the subject may respond with more than one word. Also there it is possible to have a greater flexibility and variety of responses and more area of personality and experiences may be tapped.

In addition to the projective techniques mentioned above there are some others which may prove useful in many situations. These are play technique, drawing and painting tests, etc. Both of these techniques are very useful in the case of small children. In the former, the examiner observes the spontaneous behaviour of the children while playing or constructing something with the help of given material and in the latter, the natural free hand drawing and paintings of the children are the matter of the study. Both of these techniques provide a good opportunity for the careful analysis of a child's personality.

Evaluation of Projective Techniques

Merits: Projective techniques have some outstanding features which give them some sort of superiority over the other techniques of assessing the personality. They are given below.

1. The nature of appraisals being made by these techniques is usually well-disguised. The subject is, ordinarily, not aware of the true purpose of the test and even if he has knowledge, he cannot know what aspects of his responses are significant or what significance they have. Therefore, there is no danger of distortion of the response or to give selective responses by the subject.

2. In these projective techniques, the tasks presented to the individual are usually both somewhat novel and quite unstructured. The subject cannot depend upon an established, conventional and stereotyped pattern of responses. He is to respond quite independently. Therefore, by these techniques, we can be saved from the danger of practice and coaching effects from which most tests suffer.

3. Scope and area of their application is very wide. They make little or no demand on literacy or academic skills and are equally useful for children as well as adults.

4. Most of the essential aspects of the unconscious behaviour, of which the subject himself has no knowledge, can be revealed through these techniques. In this way, these techniques play a great role in disclosing the private world of the subject and hence have a unique advantage of evaluating the total personality of an individual.

Limitations: With all these good points at their credit, the projective techniques also suffer from some weaknesses. They are:

(i) Standardised projective tests are costly. Also there is shortage of such tests.

(ii) The standardised work suffers from many weaknesses. Proper norms and objective interpretation are hardly available for these tests. Also they are not highly reliable and valid.

(iii) They are time consuming both in administration and scoring.

(iv) The interpretation task is subjective and needs well-trained and experienced persons, who are, generally not available.

But these above mentioned limitations on the part of projective techniques do not make them less significant. In fact, with the essential training and knowledge at his command an expert evaluation is sure to gain very important information about the subject, not otherwise available. On the other side, it is also true that the projective techniques alone are not the answer to all questions regarding the behavioural outcomes of the individuals. These should also be supplemented with other techniques and tools of evaluating the behavioural outcomes of the student belonging to cognitive, conative and affective domain of their behaviour.

Sociometry as a Tool for Qualitative Evaluation

Etymologically the word sociometry is known to be derived from the two Latin words, "Socious" (meaning social) and "metrum" (meaning measure). Consequently, as a word meaning, it stands for a way or approach of measuring the degree of sociability or relatedness among people. It was the famous psychologist and sociologist Jacob. Levy Moreno who coined the term sociometry and used the sociometric techniques to assign residents of the New York State Training School for Girls to various residential cottages. On the basis of his study, he found that assignment on the basis of sociometry substantially reduced the number of runaways from the facility (Moreno, 1953, p. 527).

Apart from the research studies conducted by Moreno, many other sociologists and psychologists have also tried later on to study the phenomena of sociometry and use of sociometic techniques. As a result of such work, a few definitions of these techniques have come into lime light. Let us here know about a few of them.

Criswell: Sociometry is a methodology for tracking the energy vectors of interpersonal relationships in a group. It shows the patterns of how individuals associate with each other when acting as a group toward a specified end or goal (Criswell in Moreno, 1960, p. 140)

Encyclopaedia Britannica: Sociometric techniques refer to the main measurement techniques used in social psychology, in sociology and sometimes in social anthropology and psychiatry based on the assessment of social choice and interpersonal attractiveness.

Adams and Schvaneveldt: Sociometric techniques comprise the measure designed to access interaction patterns among close associates in a variety of group. Questions such as, "whom do you like best", "with whom would you rather sit", or "with whom would you rather go to the movies?" represent items frequently used to generate important data on social relationship in such groups and the expectations held by members in the group (1991, p.165).

In this way, as revealed by the definitions provided above, sociometry and sociometric techniques provide an appropriate measure for the assessment of the degree of social nearness or distance between or among the members of a social group on the basis of the choices made by them in interpersonal relationships. The task of making choices for their interrelationship in the group is thus the central factor in the art of sociometry. Commenting further on this aspect Moreno (1953, p. 720) writes:

> *"Choices are fundamental facts in all ongoing human relations, choices of people and choices of things. It is immaterial whether the motivations are known to the chooser or not; it is immaterial whether (the choices) are inarticulate or highly expressive, whether rational or irrational. They do not require any special justification as long as they are spontaneous and true to the self of the chooser."*

In the sociometry thus people as members of the group make spontaneous choices based on their own likes and dislikes, attraction and repulsions revealed in their relationships with other members of the group. These choices, then speak by themselves the preferences for "where to sit or stand"; "who is a friend or not", who is central to the group or "who is rejected and isolated" etc. preparing a solid ground for the measurement of the quality of interaction among the members of a group.

How to Make Use of Sociometry or Sociometric Techniques

1. In a group situation, the members of the group are gathered to make choices (choose others in the group) based on some or the other specific criterion (e.g. with whom would you like to move on a picnic?).

2. Group members are then asked to list their choices or preferences serially as 1, 2, 3, 4, etc. They are free to provide their choices in the minimum or maximum numbers as they like. Before starting their work they are provided necessary instructions like below:

(i) You may choose only one member of the group.
(ii) You must necessarily choose some one.
(iii) You are free to choose as many members of the group as for providing your preferences from top to bottom.

3. After that it is ensured that everyone in the group makes choices. It is also to be cared that everyone remains in a position to describe (if asked) why of his choices.

4. From the choices of all the members of the group now a description gets emerged that may be able to provide a full sketch of the networks of relationship inside the group.

The data related with those networks of relationships can be displayed as a table or matrix of each member's choices. Such a table or matrix is called a sociomatrix.

We can also present this Networks data through a map or inter connection linked drawing called as sociogram. How these two-sociomatrix and sociogram may appear in a sociometric study to communicate the types of interrelations existing with in a group and what conclusions can likely to be derived out of such graphical presentation of the interrelations can be properly visualized through the following discussion and presentation of an experimental study conducted by the author of this text.

An Experimental Study Involving Sociometric Techniques

Object	:	To find out the Social Structure of a group by means of a Sociogram.
Material	:	A Sociability Questionnaire.
Technique used	:	Moreno's Sociometric technique.
Preliminaries	:	
Subject	:	*A group of 8 Girl Students of Govt. Girls Senior Secondary School. Home Science Practical class; Rohtak.*
Age:		16+ **Date:** 20 January 2010

Description of the tool: The Sociability questionnaire consists of positive and negative questions regarding preferences for companions of the group for a specific purpose. For example, through positive questions the pupils may be asked to name the first and second preferences next to whom they would like to sit at lunch or in the classroom or with whom they would like to attend the movies or with whom they would like to work on a class project. In negative questions, they may be asked to name their first and second preferences with whom they would like least (or not like) to sit or attend movies or work on a class-project.

Where the positive questions attempt to describe attraction between the individuals by asking them to indicate whom they would choose in a specific situation; the negative questions attempt to describe repulsion between the individuals by asking them to indicate whom they would reject in a given situation. In the present questionnaire for example they were asked to name three pupils of their group whom they would prefer to work on a class-project.

Procedure: After making the students seated comfortably; the questionnaire was distributed. Through illustration they were made to understand the procedure of responding to the questions. They were also informed about the time limit in responding to all the questions in the questionnaire. They were asked to write down the names of students, in order of 1st and 2nd preferences belonging to the present group.

Analysis of the Responses: The responses given by the students for a specific situation were tabulated as below in the form of a Sociometric matrix. Here we have taken the situation where they have been asked to give their preferences to indicate with whom they would prefer to work on a class-project.

Table 3.2: Sociometric Matrix Showing Who Chooses Whom for Working on a Class Project

Chooser	A	B	C	D	E	F	G	H
A		I		II				
B			I	II	II			
C		I						
D		I	II					
E		I						II
F							II	
G		II			I			I
H		II			I			
I choice		4	1	0	2	0	0	1
II choice		2	1	2	1	0	1	1
Total	**0**	**6**	**2**	**2**	**3**	**0**	**1**	**2**

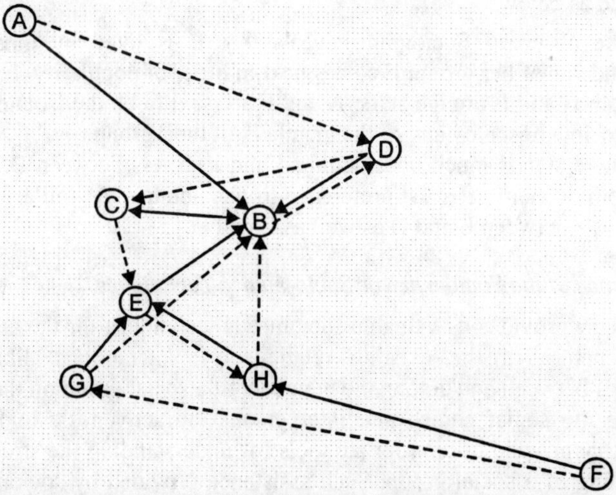

Fig. 3.3: Sociogram showing I and II choices as tabulated in the Sociometric Matrix. I and II choices have been shown by complete and dotted lines respectively

Interpretation Techniques of the Sociogram

The arrow directed to a person signifies attraction or choice made for him/her by the person at the place of which the arrow has emerged. In this way, the person who receives maximum arrows directed towards him/her is referred to as Sociometric Star, the most popular and liked one in the networks of relationships existing in the group. The emergence and direction of the other arrows may be interpreted in some other ways like below:

- When incoming and outgoing directions of arrows emerges between two persons in the sociogram, it indicates that these two persons like and choose each other and the relationship existing between them is mutual.
- The directions of the arrows may also indicate the existence of a chain type relationship among the members of the group in case we find in a sociogram that A has chosen B, who has chosen C, who has chosen D and so on.
- There may also exist clear gaps or cleavages in the sociogram in case clusters of the persons in a group are seen to choose each other but no one in any cluster has chosen anyone in any other cluster. This phenomenon in sociogram is to be interpreted as there exists no clear cut isolations between various sub groups.

Interpretation of the Present Sociogram

The sociogram obtained in the present study is capable of revealing various facts related to the social structure of the group. The important ones may be described as below:

(i) The observed Sociogram reveals that B is liked by most of the students of her group. E comes next in order of popularity. In this way both B and E are the stars. A and F are said to be the isolates as they are not chosen by any of the members of their group.

(ii) There stands much understanding and nearness between B and C as both of them offer 1st preference to one another. A similar bond also exists between E and H as well as B and D.

Importance of the Sociometry or Socio-metric Techniques

Sociometry provides us valuable sociometric techniques for the assessment of the nature of the existing relationships, interactions, likings and dislikings between and among the members of a social group on the basis of studying the social choice and interpersonal attractiveness. In fact, thus sociometry provide us appropriate tools for understanding the structure and functioning of a social group. Such assistance provided by sociometry can prove helpful to us in a variety of ways like below in the school classroom, laboratory, excursions/field trips, guidance and counselling, group training and therapeutic situations.

1. It can help us to locate performance stars in a particular learning and work environment. We can thus have popular leaders, brilliant monitors,

actors and workers for helping us in the organization of various types of curricular and co-curricular activities in a proper way.

2. It can help us to locate smaller groups of similar likings, mutual trust and attraction. In our organisation and conducting various academic activities and co-curricular activities, we most often in needs of such small groups where student can work and produce something as a most cohesive social unit. Here the sociogram findings can prove us quite useful in achieving better results.

3. In can help us to locate the cases of mutual distrust, conflicts, non-communication, rivalry, etc. existing between and among the members of the group. Sociometry and its techniques, in their unique way of collecting data and interpretation, can then prove quite powerful tool in the timely diagnosis of the weaknesses and malfunctioning prevalent in the social structure and functioning of the social groups utilized for formal or informal education. With such diagnosis now, proper remedial steps can be taken for reducing conflicts and bringing improvement in the interpersonal relationships, communications and cooperative learning or working situations.

4. The study of relationships through sociometry can prove quite helpful for the teachers, trainers, guidance and counselling personnel to collect necessary data for providing group guidance, teaching and training to the students in the group including group therapy at the hands of psychiatrists and psychologists.

5. The knowledge gained from the sociometric techniques prove quite helpful in helping the students as members of the social group (school, classroom, laboratory, workshop, hostel, tours and excursions groups, etc.) in their co-existence, peaceful living, cooperative learning or working with each other by getting rid of them with the problem of rivalry, mutual distrust and maladjustment. A simple problem of living in the dormitories of a hostel can be solved by allotting seats on the basis of sociometry findings.

6. The sociometric findings can prove quite helpful in the proper organization of the group work related to formal and informal teaching and learning. The planning and execution of the working in the tasks like team teaching, cooperative learning, project work, group assignment, team work in the co curricular activities — sports, games, dance, drama, visits or excursions, etc. can be appropriately done in case we give due consideration to the choices made and attractions existed between and among the social groups and sub-groups used by us for the formal and informal education.

In this way, sociometry and sociometric techniques can prove quite helpful and worthwhile for us in arranging and organising tasks and activities (whether formal or informal) in various group situations in an appropriate group learning or working environment for the realization of the ultimate welfare of the individual and group as a whole.

Use of Evaluation Tools for Internal Assessment and Maintaining Cumulative Records

The term internal assessment stands for the assessment or evaluation carried out purely on internal basis and thus making it as an internal affair of the institution. The introduction of the scheme of internal assessment in the system of school education, thus requires that the task of measurement and evaluation should be planned, developed, implemented and made into use by the school personnel mostly for serving their own interests including the internal educational purposes of the institution.

The question may arise then, why the evaluation task of the achievement and performance is needed to be worked out by an internal system maintained in the school. The reason in support is quite simple and straight forward. The school personnel, teachers, laboratory and workshop personnel, head of the institution and co-curricular activities incharges are the persons entrusted with the responsibilities of bringing desired changes in the behaviour of pupils for their proper growth and development. They have to provide the needed experiences for the students for this purpose. It is but natural, that these personnels must have a continuous information and feedback about their efforts. It can be only known through the testing, assessment and measurement of the student's behavioural changes, achievement and performances. It is why they should feel a requirement of having a proper cognition and feedback of the outputs of their students in its proper continuity. Needs of a person can be better served if he makes his own attempts for serving his needs. It is here the attempts made by school personnel in terms of planning and executing their own system of internal evaluation are called for. Moreover, they are the persons who remain in touch with the students most of the time. They are the one who are able to keep a close watch, observation and supervision of the student's behaviour and activities. It can thus very well concluded that no outside agency or expert can match them in their capacities, devotion and time giving for doing best in the interest and welfare of the students.

The internal evaluation work carried out by the school personnel has an additional advantages over any system maintained with the outside agency or personnel in the sense, that it may prove quite handy, convenient, economical and practicable to the school for achieving the larger purposes of the process and outcomes of evaluation. It can help in controlling all types of educational efforts, the quality of material and human resources including students for uplifting the cause of providing better education and facilities to the students.

Maintenance of Cumulative Record — Nature and Need

Cumulative record, as the name suggests, represents a total and comprehensive permanent and confidential record of the cumulated educational growth and all round development of the individual student starting from the beginning of his educational career till the present stage. It is infact a complete history and pen picture of the journey travelled by "an individual student with respect to his educational attainments and growth and development of his personality along with some necessary information about his family and home back ground.

Maintenance of cumulative records of the students in school proves a big helping hand in the task of welfare and progress of the students. Emphasizing the need of their maintenance secondary education commission (1952-53) has commented in the following words.

> "*Neither the external examination nor the internal examination singly or together, can give a complete and correct picture of pupil's all round progress at any particular stage of his education, yet it is important for us to assess this in order to determine his future course of study or future vocation. For this purpose a proper system of school records should be maintained for every pupil indicating the work done by him in the school from day to day, month to month, term to term and year to year. Such school records will present a clear and continuous statement of the attainment of the child in different intellectual pursuits throughout the successive stages of his education.*"

Through the above lines in this way, secondary education commission has emphasized to maintain the educational history of the individual students. However here it has only stressed upon developing his history in terms of his attainment in different intellectual pursuits. This dimension needs to be extended to the attainments in other fields, physical, social, emotional and ethical accounting for the complete all round development brought in the personality of the student through the process of education. Then and then only we can know what the student is in himself.

In the light of the above said comprehensive nature of the maintenance of cumulative records of the students of particular school, we may now see that the format used for maintaining such record is found and consist of the following sub-divisions.

A. *Identifying data* of the students indicating his name, the name of the school, age, gender, class, his home address, etc.

B. *School history* showing the names and periods of the previous schools attended.

C. *Family and home background* indicating socio-economic status of the family education of the parents, type of family — joint or single — position of the child in the family, religion and other important things regarding the family.

D. School attendance year wise in the present school.

E. Physical/Medical Report of status of the child.

F. Scholastic achievement in all the subjects of the school curriculum in the previous as well as present year based on the internal as well as external assessment (half yearly and annually)

G. Performance in various co-curricular activities including games and sports.
H. Personality traits indicating intellectual, social, emotion and moral development of the student.
I. General remarks indicating anything special about the growth development and potential of the student.

From the above description of the internal assessment and cumulative records, we may now clearly visualize the role and significance of the various quantitative and qualitative evaluation tools in the maintenance of the system of internal assessment and cumulative records in a particular school.

Use in Carrying out Internal Assessment

The continuation of the programme of internal assessment essentially requires the need of carrying out a system of continuous and comprehensive evaluation with the help of quantitative and qualitative tools in the number of ways and forms specified as below.

1. The daily, weekly and monthly tests taken in the class by the subject teachers for accessing the achievement and performance of the students.
2. The terminal, half yearly and annual examinations organised and held by the school with the help of teacher made or standardized test.
3. The questions put in the classrooms and answers given to these questions by the students.
4. The record of the evaluation of the drill work, home work assignment given to the students.
5. The record of the practice and practical work done by the students through the help of practical examinations conducted from time to time.
6. The record of the work demonstrating the constructive and creative potential of the students.
7. Day to day observation and evaluation of the performance of the students in respect of the classroom teaching-learning activities *i.e.* actively responding to the questions put in the class, remaining quite active in the learning process, playing active and appropriate role in classroom discussion and providing evidence of their active participation, alertness and achievement in one or the other ways. (Teachers may use observation, rating scales, or schedules for this purpose).
8. The record of the students in relation to his habit and quality of library reading.
9. Evaluation of the students work and performance in relation to their doing practical work in the laboratory and workshop.
10. The evaluation of the contributions and performances of the students in relation to various co-curricular activities, games and sports, NSS and Scouting, organisation of fairs and exhibition, visits to places of educational interests, community activities and school functions.

11. The record of the evaluation of the changes brought in the affective domain and personality development. (These can be evaluated by the appropriate techniques and devices like observation sociometry rating scale, interview, personality inventory and other measures of personality development, interest and attitude scales, adjustment inventories etc.)

Use of Maintaining Cumulative Record

The data regarding the educational history and performance of the student in various stages and areas of his growth and development and expected progress can be only obtained through the results or outcomes the various measures carried out though various quantitative and qualitative evaluation tools from time and time in the schools. The system of continuous and comprehensive evaluation maintained through the use of properly employed quantitative and qualitative tools in the shape of achievement tests, day to day observation of the student's behaviour, specifically designed evaluation measures for the assessment of the student's progress in cognitive, affective and conative domains of his behaviour and personality dimensions may help the teachers and school authorities to supply essential data and information for being put up in the cumulative records of the students.

4

Statistics in Educational Evaluation

Meaning of Statistics

Usually the word statistics carries the following three common meanings:

1. In the first place, it refers to numerical facts. State as well as Central, Statistical department and various other agencies can be seen engaged in collecting valuable statistics (numerical facts) concerning the birth and death, school attendance, employment market, output of industrial plants and agriculture fields, etc.

2. As a second meaning, the word statistics refers to the method or methods of dealing with numerical facts. In this sense statistics is taken as science of collecting, classifying, summarizing, analysing and interpreting of numerical facts.

3. In its third meaning statistics refers to the summarized figures of numerical facts such as percentages, averages, means, medians, modes, standard deviations etc. Each of these figures separately, (average or mean etc.) is referred to as "Statistics".

In this way the word statistics can be referred to numerical facts or science or methodology of dealing with numerical facts or summarized figures of numerical facts. Tate (1955: 5) has beautifully summarized these different meanings of the word statistics in the following witty comments, "It's all perfectly clear: you compute statistics (mean, median, mode, etc) from statistics (numerical facts) by statistics (statistics as a science or methodology)."

It is all about the different meanings that can be attached to the word "statistics". But in general sense as a subject or branch of knowledge statistics is defined as *one of the subjects of study that helps us in the scientific collection, presentation, analysis and interpretation of numerical facts.*

Need and Importance of Statistics in Educational Evaluation

Statistics, in general, renders valuable services in the following dimensions:

(a) In the collection of evidence or facts (numerical or otherwise).

(b) In the classification, organisation and summarization of numerical facts.

(c) In drawing general conclusions and inferences or making predictions on the basis of particular facts and evidences.

On account of the above mentioned services statistics is now regarded as an indispensable instrument in the field of Educational assessment especially where any sort of measurement or evaluation is involved. Its need in Education can be summarized as below:

1. In the construction and standardization of various tests and measures. Statistical methods help in the construction and standardization of various tests and measures like Achievement tests in various subjects. Intelligence tests, Aptitude tests, Interest Inventories, Attitude Scales and various other measures of personality assessment.

2. In making proper use of the results of various tests and measures. Scores obtained from various tests and measures arc always relative and not absolute. Hence, they are meaningless in themselves. Statistical methods help in their proper presentation, comparison and interpretation. This service rendered by statistics help us:

(i) to know individual differences of our students,
(ii) to render guidance to the students,
(iii) to compare the suitability of one method or technique over the other,
(iv) to compare the results of one system of evaluation with the other,
(v) to compare the function and working of one institution with the other,
(vi) to make prediction regarding the future progress of the students,
(vii) to make selection, classification and promotion of the students,
(viii) to keep various types of records and furnish Educational statistics etc.

By the above services of statistics in Educational assessment, it can be easily concluded that it is very helpful to the teachers in the proper functioning of their various duties. It gives a definite direction of the process of teaching and learning and helps the teacher to realise the broader aims and objectives of education. By its increasing popularity in Psychological as well as educational researches, it is now going to be most indispensable to every teacher. Its knowledge not only helps a teacher in acquainting with the new innovations and researches in the field of education but also prepares him to become an active participant in introducing as well as bringing changes in the field of Education.

5

Organisation and Graphical Presentation of Data

The Meaning of Term Data

The dictionary meaning of the word data is facts (plural of datum, meaning fact). Thus, in wider sense the term data designates the evidence or facts for describing a group or a situation, but in a particular sense it is generally used for numerical facts such as heights, weights, scores on achievement tests and intelligence tests, etc.

Methods of Organising and Presenting Data

The data from tests and experiments in the form of scores need to be classified and organised in a systematic way for understanding the meaning and deriving some useful conclusions. In general the following four methods are used for organising and presenting statistical data:

A. Presentation in the form of Statistical Tables.
B. Presentation in the form of Frequency Distribution.
C. Graphical presentation of Ungrouped Data.
D. Graphical presentation of Frequency distribution (Grouped Data)

A. Statistical Tables

In this form of presentation, the data are tabulated or arranged in some properly selected classes, and the arrangement is described by title and sub-titles. Such tables can list the original raw scores as well as the percentages, means, standard deviations, etc. Below we give a sketch of table for illustration.

Table 5.1: Pass Percentages of High Schools of Rohtak City in the High School Public Examination

	Name of the School	*Pass percentage*	*Girls Pass percentage*	*Boys Pass percentage*
High School of Rohtak	A			
	B			
	C			
	D			
	E			

B. Frequency Distribution

In this form of presentation, we group the quantitative data into some arbitrarily chosen classes For this purpose, usually, the scores are distributed into groups of scores (classes) and each score is allotted a place in the respective group or class. It is also seen how many times a particular score or group of scores occurs in the given data. This is known as the frequency of a score or group of scores. In this way, *Frequency distribution may be considered as a method of presenting a collection of groups of scores in such a way as to show the frequency in each group of scores or class.* Various steps for presenting quantitative data by a frequency distribution can be understood properly with the help of the following example:

Example 5.1: The marks obtained by 50 students in an Achievement test are given below—

62	21	26	32	56	36	37	39	53	40	54	42
44	61	68	28	33	56	57	37	52	39	40	54
43	43	63	30	34	58	35	38	50	38	52	41
51	44	41	42	43	45	46	45	47	48	49	45
46	48										

Tabulate these scores in a Frequency distribution by clearly explaining the various steps involved.

Steps for Grouping Data into Frequency Distribution

1. Finding the range. First of all the range of the series to be grouped is found out. It is done by subtracting the lowest score from the highest. In this present problem the range of the distribution is 68–21 *i.e.* 47.

2. To determine the class interval or grouping interval. After finding out the range, the number and size of the classes or groups to be used in grouping the data are decided.

There exists two different rules for this purpose:

First Rule: For gaining an idea of the size of the classes *i.e.* class interval, the range is divided by the number of classes desired. Class interval is usually denoted by the symbol 'i' and is always a whole number. Thus, the formula for deciding the class interval is—

$$i = \frac{\text{Range}}{\text{Number of Classes Desired}}$$

Now the question arises in how many classes or groups one should distribute given data. As a general rule Tate writes, "If the series contains fewer than about 50 items, more than about 10 classes are not justified. If the series contains from about 50 to 100 items, 10 to 15 classes tend to be appropriate; if more than 100 items. 15 or more classes tend to be appropriate. Ordinarily, not fewer than 10 classes or more than 20 are used." (1955. p. 44)

If by dividing Range by number of classes we do not get a whole number, the nearest, appropriate number is taken as class interval.

Second Rule: According to the second rule class interval (i) is first decided and then the number of the classes is determined. For this purpose, usually, the class intervals of 2, 3, 5 or 10 units in length are used.

Both of the above mentioned rules are practised. In our opinion, it is better to use a combined procedure made out of both the rules. Actually the range, the number of classes and the class interval — all should be taken into consideration while planning for a frequency distribution and we must aim to select a proper class interval (*i*) that can yield, appropriate categories (number of classes) as mentioned above by Tate.

Considering in this way, the proper class interval (*i*) in the present example is 5.

(Here Range = 47. Scores are 50 in number and thus about 10 classes are sufficient. Therefore $i = 47/10 = 4.7$ *i.e.* Nearest whole number = 5).

3. Writing the Content of Frequency Distribution: After deciding the size and number of the class interval and locating the highest and lowest scores of the given data, we proceed to write down the contents of the Frequency distribution. For this purpose 3 columns are drawn and work is carried out as under:

(a) *Writing the classes of distribution.* In the first column, we write down all the classes of distribution. For this purpose first of all the lowest class is settled down and afterwards other subsequent classes are written down. In the present problem 20—24 can be taken as the lowest class and then we can have classes as 25—29. 30—34, etc. upto 65–69.

(b) *Tallying the Scores into proper classes*: Under this step, the scores given in the data are taken one by one and tallied in their proper classes as shown in the 2nd column of the table given below. These tally marks against each class are then counted. These counted numbers are respectively called the frequencies of that class. They are written in the third column as shown below:

Table 5.2

Class of Scores	*Tallies*	*Frequencies*
65-69	I	1
60-64	III	3
55-59	IIII	4
50-54	IIII II	7
45-49	IIII IIII	9
40-44	IIII IIII I	11
35-39	IIII III	8
30-34	IIII	4
25-29	II	2
20-24	I	1
	Total Frequencies (N)	**50**

(c) *Checking the tallies*: The total of 3rd column should be equal to the number of individuals whose scores have been tabulated. Under the above tabulation total of frequencies *i.e.* 50 agrees with the total number of students given in the problem.

Some more things to be known regarding a Frequency Distribution

1. *Class limits of the frequency distribution.* The designation of classes *i.e.* 20—24. 25—29. 30—34, etc. are called the indicated or written class limits. The actual class limits are always taken as 0.5 units below and 0.5 units above the written class limits. For example, the actual limit of class 20–24 is 19.5—24.5 (19.5 as lower and 24.5 as higher class limits.)

2. *The Mid-point of a class in a frequency distribution.* In a frequency distribution classes are sometimes indicated by their mid-values or mid-points. The formula of determining the mid-point of a class is—

Mid-point of a class = Indicated or written lower limit
+ [(upper limit – lower limit)/2]

(*Note.* We don't consider actual class limits in calculating mid-point. Thus, of the class 20—24 the mid-point is 20 + [24—20/2] = 20 + 2 = 22.

C. Graphical Representation of Ungrouped Data

For the data which is not grouped into a frequency distribution we use the following common graphs or diagrams.

(i) Pictographs or Pictograms
(ii) Bar graphs on Bar Diagrams.
(iii) Circle or Pie graphs/diagrams
(iv) Line graphs.

Let us have an idea of all these four types of graphical representation.

Pictographs or Pictograms: Pictographs or pictograms are the graphs or diagrams used for presenting an ungrouped statistical data in a pictorial (picture like) form. A picture is said to be worth more than 100 words spoken or written. Thereby the pictorial representation of the data is always considered better than its description in the words and figures. Let us illustrate this fact through an example.

Example 5.2. In a physical efficiency test 100 students cleared from district A, 85 students from district B, 80 students from district C, 90 students from district D and 70 students from district E. Present data first into a tabulation form and then in pictorial form.

Solution: Presentation of data in a Tabular Form **Table 5.3**.

District	A	B	C	D	E
Number of Students	100	85	80	90	70

Presentation of Data in the Pictorial Form

Step 1. Let us decide to represent a student with a picture (indicative of a student figure)

Step 2. For the sake of brevity and simplicity let us have a scale, a picture (of student) equal to 20 students in number.

Following these steps the pictorial presentation (pictograph) of the given data will be as under—

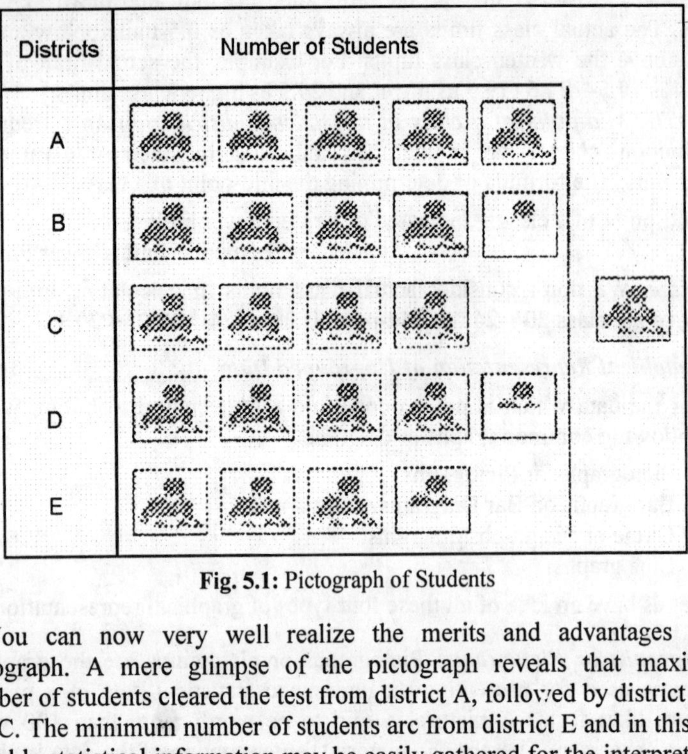

Fig. 5.1: Pictograph of Students

You can now very well realize the merits and advantages of a pictograph. A mere glimpse of the pictograph reveals that maximum number of students cleared the test from district A, followed by district D, B and C. The minimum number of students arc from district E and in this way valuable statistical information may be easily gathered for the interpretation of test results in an interesting and pleasing way from a pictograph.

However, there lies some difficulties in the pictorial presentation of data especially in choosing a suitable scale (picture for a given number of units) and its comprehension. In the above two examples we have chosen figure of student representing strength 20. In this pictograph we may easily notice the difficulties encountered in representing the numbers not wholly divisible by 20 *i.e.* 30, 50, 70, 85, 90, etc. We have represented the strength of 85 students with four complete picture and fraction (only head). Here we just have approximation and not the exact measurement of the pictorial figures for representing the scaled fractions numerical data. This difficulty can be somewhat removed in other forms of graphical representation of data as will be noticed soon.

Bar Graphs or Bar Diagrams: Instead of using pictures we can use bars (rectangles of similar breadth) for the representation of numerical data. This mode of presentation statistical data through bars is known as bar graphs or bar diagrams. As example let us try to have a bar graph of the tabulated data given in example 5.1. It may take the following shape given in the Fig. 5.2.

How to draw Bar Graph?

(i) Try to use a graph paper for drawing the bar graph.

(ii) On one of the axes X or Y try to plot numerical data by choosing a proper scale and have the other variable like classes in this example on the other axis. Here in this example the numerical strength of students has been plotted on the y-axis. Here the number of students in the different classes are thus represented by the bars (rectangles of similar breadth) constructed on the x-axis.

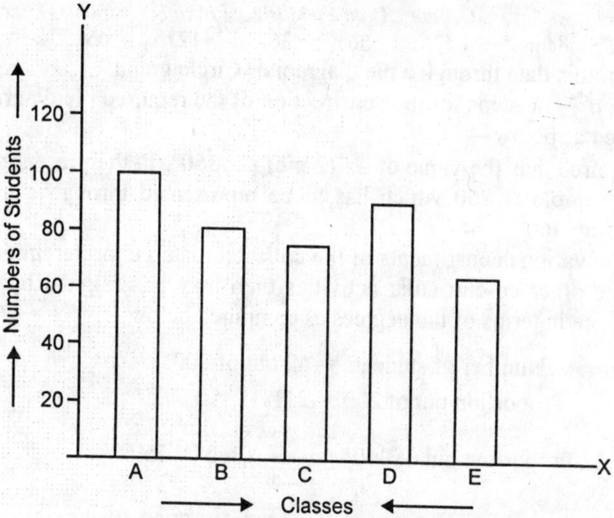

Fig. 5.2: Bar graph or Bar diagram showing the strength of students passed the efficiency test.

What can be inferred from the Bar Graph?

A bar graph just shown above in the figure 5.2 may provide the following information in a quite simple and speedy way.

- It shows the strength of students cleared the test belonging to a particular district *i.e.* 70 students cleared the test from district E.
- The district having highest strength of the students cleared the test in district A.
- The district having lowest strength of the students cleared the test in district E.
- The relative strengths of the students clearing the test from different

districts of the state may also be adjudged easily for one or the other type of comparisons.

***Circle Graph or Pie Diagrams*:** Circle or pie graphs/diagrams provide us an opportunity to represent statistical data through the figure or a circle and its constituents *i.e.* proportionate sub-divisions. These are specifically helpful in the case for which the question of proportion is of much interest. To construct them requires a working knowledge of angle measurement and percentages.

The process of the construction of a pie graph may be understood with the help of an example given below.

Example 5.3: 200 students of a Students' hobby club were asked to give their options for the participation in one or the other types of co-curricular activities. The preferences data was tabulated as under:

Activities	*Debate*	*Dance*	*Music*	*Painting*	*Models*	*Excursion*
Number of Students	42	36	36	12	6	68

Present this data through a pie diagram or Circle graph.

Solution—The steps for the construction of the required pie diagram may be outlined as below—

(i) A circle has the value of 2π (2 pie) *i.e.* 360°. In the present example the total sample is 200 which has to be represented through a complete circle having 360°.

(ii) The various constituents of the collected data *i.e.* preferences for the one or the other co-curricular activities then may be assigned by varying values of pie in terms of the degrees as computed below—

Debate: Number of students = 42 out of 200

Proportion out of 200 = 21%

$$42 \text{ Proportion out of } 360° = \frac{42}{200} \times 360° = 75.6°$$

Dances and Music: No. of Students = 36 out of 200

$$\text{Proportion out of } 200 = \frac{36}{200} \times 100 = 18\%$$

$$\text{Proportion out of } 360° = \frac{36}{200} \times 360° = 64.8°$$

Painting: No. of Students = 12 out of 200

$$\text{Proportion out of } 200 = \frac{12}{200} \times 100 = 6\%$$

$$\text{Proportion out of } 360° = \frac{12}{200} \times 360° = 21.6°$$

Modelling: No. of Students 6 out of 200

$$\text{Proportion out of } 200 = \frac{6}{200} \times 100 = 3\%$$

$$\text{Proportion out of } 360° = \frac{6}{200} \times 360° = 10.8°$$

Excursion: No. of Students = 68 out of 200

$$\text{Proportion out of } 200 = \frac{68}{200} \times 100 = 34\%$$

$$\text{Proportion out of } 360° = \frac{68}{200} \times 360° = 122.4°$$

(iii) Now all these above proportions 75.6°, 64.8°, 64.8°, 21.6°, 10.8° and 122.4° may be represented as the different sectors of a whole circle with the help of the knowledge concerning measurement of angels.

(iv) These may take the final following form for making the required pie diagram.

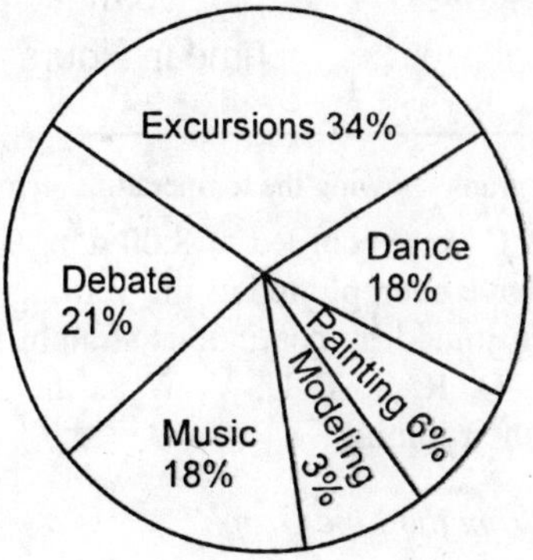

Fig. 5.3: Pie Graph showing preferences of students for the co-curricular activities

***Line Graphs*:** Line graphs can be better used in describing the con-committed relationships between two variables by plotting their respective values on the x and y axes of a graph paper (After choosing appropriate scales). Let us illustrate this fact through examples.

Example 5.4: Science students of the IX class of a school collected data about weather on a cold day of the month December by recording the room temperature at various hours of the day and obtained the following line graph of the results of their survey.

Process of Construction

(i) Here time in hours has been plotted on x-axis and the corresponding temperature in centigrade have been plotted on y-axis.

(ii) The five small squares of the graph papers have been taken equivalent to 1 hour on x-axis and 2 centigrades on y-axis.

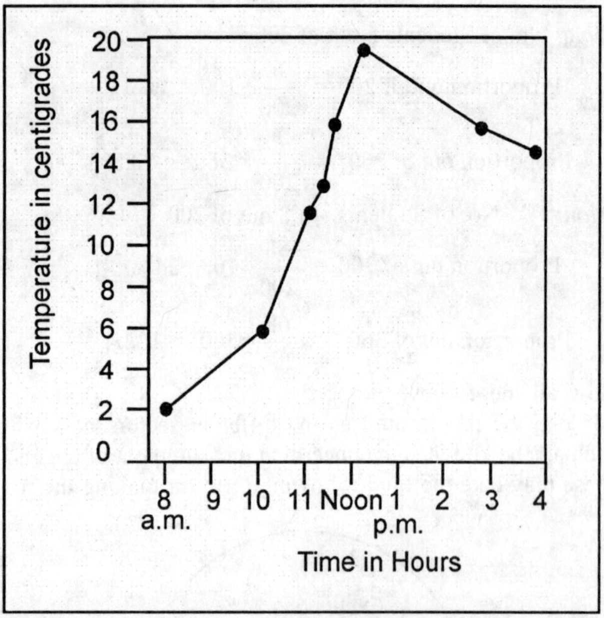

Fig. 5.4: A line graph showing the temperature on a December day.

(iii) The facts like 2°C was recorded at 8.00 a.m. 0.6°C was recorded at 10.00 a.m. etc. have been plotted as the varying points and then these points have been joined by continuous straight lines (see the placing of the points P, Q, R, S, T, U, V, W as the intersection points of paired data and their joining).

What can be inferred from the Line Graph?

Line graphs like above can reveal many facts and information about the collected data and consequently we may be able to get answers of the queries like below—

1. For which hours during the day did the students collect data?
2. What was the high temperature of the day according to the graph?
3. Between what hours was the temperature increasing or decreasing?
4. About what time in the morning was the temperature about 10°?
5. What do you predict the temperature might be at 5.00 p.m. lower than or higher than 16°C?

Example 5.5: The line graph given in Fig. 5.5 depicts mastery of multiplication facts by a particular student in the a course of learning. Here the time spent in weeks for having mastery over the multiplication facts is shown on x-axis and the achievement in terms of mastery (known through the percentage of facts mastered) is shown on y-axis by choosing appropriate scales.

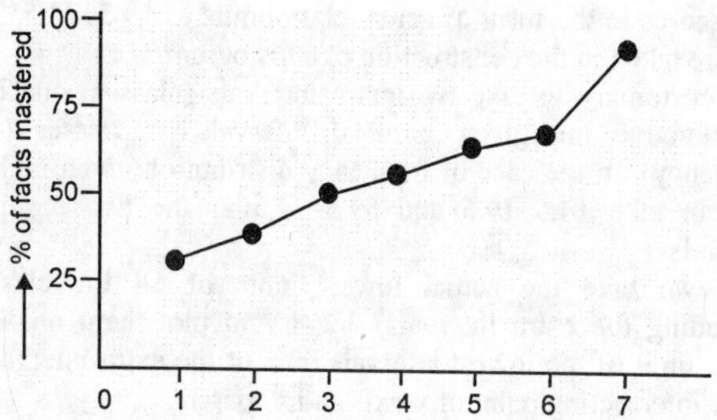

Fig. 5.5: Line Graph showing progress about mastery over the multiplication facts

Conclusion about choosing a particular graphical mode for the representation of Ungrouped Data

Each of the graphical mode, pictograph, pie graph and line graph, described above have their own merits and limitations of being utilised in the representation of a given ungrouped data at a particular occasion to furnish useful information. Therefore, a wise decision should always be made before the employment of a particular graphic mode in a particular situation. Take the last example of representing the data concerning mastery over the multiplication by a line graph. Here it would make no sense whatever to turn these weekly mastery figures into a pie or bar chart. There is also no possibility of representing these through pictograph. Similarly, in the case of representing facts concerning the percentage of participation in co-curricular activities, there will be no sense in displaying it through a line graph. Here the decision for representing the different figures through a pie graph seems quite appropriate as there stands a whole of which the different figures concerning activity choices are collectively a part. Contrarily in the case, showing concomitant changes occurred in a one variable, relation to the changes introduced in the other, it is always advisable to use line graph as the mode of representation. In this way, while trying to determine how to best display the particular data one must decide whether to graph the data, and if so, what kind of graph to use.

D. Graphical Presentation of Frequency Distribution (Grouped Data)

There are four methods of representing a frequency distribution graphically:

1. The Histogram or column diagram.
2. The Frequency Polygon.
3. The Cumulative Frequency Graph.
4. The Cumulative Frequency Percentage Curve or Ogive.

Let us discuss them one by one.

Histogram: A histogram or column diagram is essentially a bar graph of a frequency distribution. The following points are to be kept in mind while constructing the histogram for a frequency distribution:

(i) The scores in the form of actual class limits as 19.5–24.5, 24.5–29.5, etc. are taken in the construction of a histogram.

(ii) It is customary to take two extra intervals (classes) one below and other above the given grouped intervals or classes (with zero frequency). In the case of frequency distribution given in Table 13.2, we can take 14.5–19.5 and 69.5–74.5 as the two required extra-intervals.

(iii) Now we take the actual lower limits of all the class-intervals (including the extra intervals) and try to plot them on x-axis. The lower limit of the lowest intervals (one of the extra intervals is taken at the intersecting point of x-axis and y-axis.)

(iv) Frequencies of the distribution are plotted on y-axis.

(v) Each class or interval with its specific frequency is represented by a separate rectangle. The base of each rectangle is the width of the interval (*i*) and the height is the respective frequency of that class or interval.

(vi) It is not essential to project the sides of the rectangles down to the base line.

(vii) Care should be taken to select the appropriate units of representation along the x-axis and y-axis. Both x-axis as well as y-axis should not be either too short or too long. A good general rule for this purpose as suggested by Garrett "*is to select x and y units which will make the height of figures approximately 75% of its width.*" (1971, p. 11)

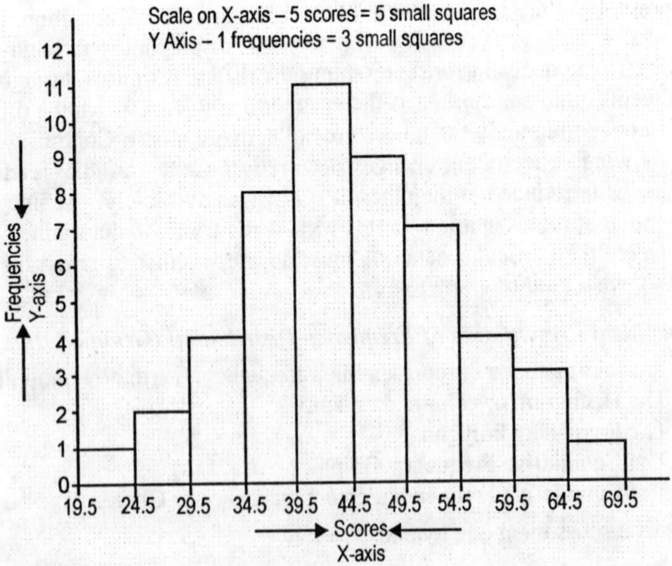

Fig. 5.6: Histogram of the Frequency Distribution Given in Table 5.2

Frequency Polygon: A Frequency polygon is essentially a line graph for the graphical representation of the frequency distribution. We can get a frequency polygon from a histogram, if the mid-points of the upper bases of the rectangles are connected. But it is not essential to plot histogram first to draw a frequency polygon. We can construct it directly from a given frequency distribution. The following points are helpful in constructing a frequency polygon:

(i) Like histogram two extra intervals or classes one above and the other below the given intervals are taken.

(ii) The mid-points of the all classes or intervals (including two extra intervals) are calculated.

(iii) The mid-points are marked along the x-axis and the corresponding frequencies are plotted along the v-axis by choosing suitable scales on both axes.

(iv) The various points obtained by plotting the mid-points and frequencies are joined by straight line to give the frequency polygon.

(v) For the approximate height of the figure and selection of x and y units the rule emphasized earlier in the case of histogram should be followed.

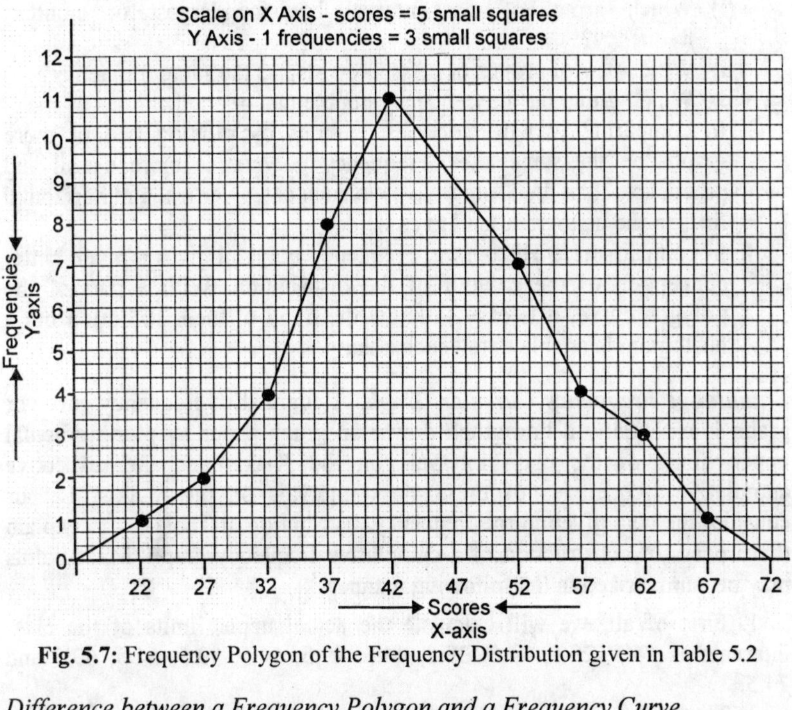

Fig. 5.7: Frequency Polygon of the Frequency Distribution given in Table 5.2

Difference between a Frequency Polygon and a Frequency Curve

A polygon is a many sided figure. It is essentially a closed curve while frequency curve is not a closed curve. In Frequency curve, we do not take two extra classes or intervals, one above and the other below the given classes. But in Frequency polygon, we take these two extra classes in order to close the figure.

Comparison between the Histogram and the Frequency Polygon

Although Histogram and Frequency polygon — both are used for the graphic representation of the frequency distribution and are alike in many aspects yet they possess points of differences. Some of these differences can be cited as below:

1. Where Histogram is essentially the bar graph of the given frequency distribution, the Frequency polygon is a line graph of this distribution.
2. In Frequency polygon we assume frequencies to be concentrated at the mid-points of the class interval. It points out merely the graphical relationship between mid-points and frequencies and thus is unable to show the distribution of frequencies within each class interval. But the Histogram gives a very clear as well as accurate picture of the relative proportions of frequency from interval to interval. A mere glimpse of the figure answers such questions as:
   (i) Which group of class-interval has the largest or smallest frequency?
   (ii) Which pair of groups or class intervals has the same frequency?
   (iii) Which group has its frequency double that of another?
3. In comparing two or more distributions by plotting two or more graphs on the same axes, Frequency polygon is more useful and practicable than the Histogram as in such cases vertical and horizontal lines in the histogram tend to coincide.
4. In comparison to Histogram, Frequency polygon gives a much better conception of the contour of the distribution. With a part of the polygon curve, it is easy to know the trend of the distribution but a Histogram is unable to tell such a thing.

Cumulative Frequency Curve or Graph: A cumulative frequency curve or graph is essentially a line graph drawn on graph paper by plotting actual upper limits of the class intervals on the X-axis and the respective cumulative frequencies of these class intervals on the Y-axis. Let us consider the data given in the frequency distribution in Table 5.4 to explain the process of construction of a cumulative frequency graph. Main points may be summarized in the following manner:

1. First of all, we will calculate the actual upper limits of the class intervals as 24.5, 29.5, 34.5, 39.5, 44.5, 49.5, 54.5, 59.5, 64.5, 69.5 and 74.5.

2. Then we will try to determine/compute cumulative frequencies and write them at the proper place against the respective class interval in the manner given ahead in the Table 5.4.

Table 5.4: Computation of Cumulative Frequencies

Class Interval	*Frequency*	*Cumulative Frequency*
65 — 69	1	50
60 — 64	3	49
55 — 59	4	46
50 — 54	7	42
45 — 49	9	35
40 — 44	11	26
35 — 39	8	15
30 — 34	4	7
25 — 29	2	3
20 — 24	1	1

As may be clear to you with the observation of the cumulative frequencies written in the third Column of the Table 5.4, cumulative frequencies are then obtained by adding successively starting from the bottom, the individual frequencies. In the given table, when we start from the bottom the first cumulative frequency is to be written as 1 against the lowest class interval, *i.e.* 20-24. Then we get 3 as another cumulative frequency by adding 1 and 2, then 7 by adding 1, 2 and 4. Similarly, by adding 1, 2, 4 and 8, we get 15 as a cumulative frequency to be written against the interval 35-39. As the actual upper limit of this class interval is 39.5, it may be safely claimed that there are 15 students in the class of 50 students whose achievement scores lie below 39.5.

3. Now, for plotting the actual upper limits of the class intervals on the X-axis and respective cumulative frequencies on the Y-axis of the graph paper, we must select a suitable scale with reference to the range of data to be plotted and the size of graph paper to be used.

4. All the plotted points representing upper limits of the class interval with their respective cumulative frequencies will then be joined through a successive chain of straight lines resulting in a line graph.

5. To plot the origin of the curve on the X-axis, it is customary to take one extra class interval with zero cumulative frequency and thus calculate the actual upper limit of this class interval, In the present case the upper limit will be 19.5. It will be the starting point of the curve.

6. Cumulative frequency curve of the frequency distribution given in Table 5.2 then will look like below as given in the Figure 5.8

Cumulative Percentage Frequency Curve or Ogive: The cumulative percentage frequency curve or Ogive is essentially a line graph drawn on a piece of graph paper by plotting actual upper limits of the class intervals on the X-axis and their respective cumulative percentage frequencies on the Y-axis. Ogive differs from the cumulative frequency graph in the sense that here we plot cumulative percentage frequencies on the Y-axis in place of cumulative frequencies. The question here may arise that how can we compute cumulative percentage frequencies.

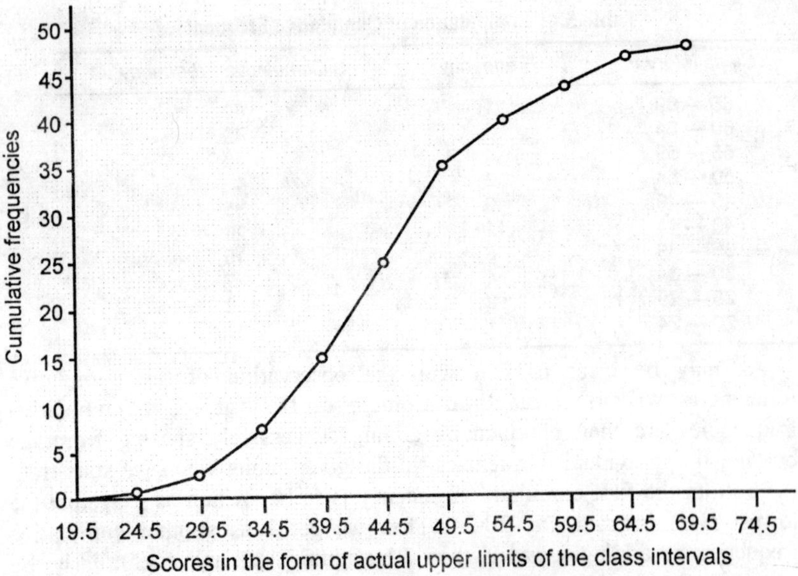

Fig. 5.8: Cumulative Frequency Curve of the Frequency Distribution given in Table 5.2

Four computing cumulative percentage frequencies of scores grouped into a frequency distribution the steps like below are followed:

(i) First we compute cumulative frequencies as discussed earlier and presented in the Table 5.3.

(ii) Then these cumulative frequencies are converted into cumulative-percentage frequencies.

For converting cumulative frequencies into cumulative percentage frequencies, the particular cumulative frequency is multiplied by 100/N where *N* is the total number of frequencies (total number of students whose achievement scores have been included in the present example). These frequencies tell us the percentage of cases lying below a given score or class limit. For example, the cumulative frequency of 15 can be converted into cumulative percentage frequency by multiplying by 100/N. *i.e.* 100/50 x 2. Thus, we obtain 30 as the cumulative percentage frequency against the class interval 35-39. This cumulative percentage frequency may help us conclude that there are 30% of students in the class of fifty, whose achievement scores lie below the score 39.5. Similarly, the cumulative percentage frequency of 70 may tell us that there are 70% of students whose scores lie below the upper limit of the class interval 45-49, *i.e.* 49.5.

(iii) After computing the cumulative percentage frequencies in the manner given above these may be arranged in the way given in Table 5.5

Table 5.5: Computation of Cumulative Percentage Frequencies

Class interval	*Frequency*	*Cumulative Frequency*	*Cumulative Percentage Frequency*
65 - 69	1	50	100 00
60 - 64	3	49	98.00
55 - 59	4	46	92.00
50 - 54	7	42	84.00
45 - 49	9	35	70.00
40 - 44	11	26	52.00
35 - 39	8	15	30.00
30 - 34	4	7	14.00
25 - 29	2	3	6.00
20 - 24	1	1	2.00

(iv) Now the actual upper limits of the class intervals are plotted on the X-axis and respective cumulative percentage frequencies are to be plotted on the Y-axis by selecting a suitable scale with reference to the range of data to be plotted and the size of the graph paper to be used.

(v) To plot the origin of the cumulative percentage frequency orgive on the X-axis, it is customary to take one extra class interval with zero cumulative percentage frequency and then calculate the actual upper limit of this extra class interval. In the present case also this upper limit (like already discussed for the cumulative frequency curve) will be 19.5. It will be starting point of the curve.

(iv) All the plotted points representing upper limits of the class interval with their respective cumulative percentage frequencies will then be joined through a successive chain of straight lines resulting into a line graph looked like as ahead (see figure 5.9)

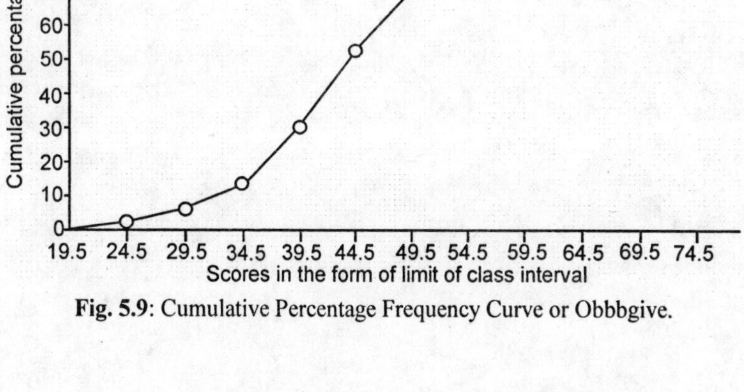

Fig. 5.9: Cumulative Percentage Frequency Curve or Obbbgive.

Use of the Cumulative Percentage Frequency Curve or Ogive

Cumulative percentage frequency curve (ogive) helps in the following tasks:

1. The statistics like median, quartiles, quartile deviations, deciles, percentiles and percentile ranks may be determined quickly and fairly accurately.
2. Percentile norms (a type of norm representing the typical performance of some designated group or groups) may be easily and accurately determined.
3. We can have an overall comparison of two or more groups or frequency distributions by plotting the ogives concerning these distributions on the same coordinate axes. A frequency curve may also be used for such comparison. The difference lies in the fact that a frequency curve is used in the case when the total frequencies (*N*) in the distributions are the same; but when the total frequencies are different, we have to draw the frequency percentage curve or ogive.

6

Measures of Central Tendency, Percentiles and Percentile Rank

Introduction

If we take the achievement scores of the students of a class and arrange them in a frequency distribution, we can easily find that there are few students who either score very high or very low. The marks of most of the students lie somewhere between the highest and the lowest scores of the whole class. This tendency of a group of distribution is named as central tendency and the typical score lying between the extremes and shared by most of the students is referred to as a measure of central tendency. In this way, a measure of central tendency as Tate defines *"is a sort of average or typical value of the items in the series and its function is to summarize the series in terms of this average value."* (1955, p. 78) The most common measures of central tendency are:

(i) Arithmetic mean or mean (ii) median and (iii) mode.

Each of them, in its own way can be called a representative of the characteristics of the whole group and thus the performance of the group as a whole can be described by the single value which each of these measures give. The values of mean, median or mode also help us in comparing two or more groups or frequency distributions in terms of typical or characteristics performance. In the following pages we will study these measures of central tendency

Arithmetic Mean (M)

It is the simplest but most useful measure of central tendency. It is nothing but the 'average' which we compute in our High School Arithmetic and therefore can be easily defined as the sum of all the values of the items in a series divided by the number of items. It is designated by the symbol M.

Computation of Mean in the Case of Ungrouped Data

Let X_1, X_2, X_3, X_4, X_5, X_6, X_7, X_8, X_9, X_{10}, be the scores obtained by 10 students in an Achievement Test. Then the Arithmetic mean or Mean scores of the group of these students can be calculated as

$$M = \frac{X_1 + X_2 + X_3 + ... + X_{10}}{10}$$

In this way, the formula for calculating mean of an ungrouped data is $M = \frac{\Sigma X}{N}$, where ΣX stands for the sum of the scores or values of the items and N for the total number of items is a series or group.

Computation of Mean in the Case of Grouped Data (Data in the Form of Frequency Distribution)

(i) In frequency distribution where frequencies are greater than 1, the mean is calculated by the formula $M = \frac{\Sigma f X}{N}$, Where X represents the mid-point of class interval, *f* its respective frequency and N, the total of all the frequencies.

We can illustrate the use of this formula by taking the frequency distribution previously given in Table No. 5.2. of Chapter 5.

Scores	*f*	*Mid-(Point) X*	*fX*
65-69	1	67	67
60-64	3	62	186
55-59	4	57	228
50-54	7	52	364
45-49	9	47	423
40-44	11	42	462
35-39	8	37	296
30-34	4	32	128
25-29	2	27	54
20-24	1	22	22
			$\Sigma f X = 2230$

$$M = \frac{\Sigma f X}{N} = \frac{2230}{50} = 44.6$$

Arithmetic mean = 44.6

(ii) Short cut method of computing the mean of grouped data

Mean for the grouped data can be computed easily with the help of the following formula: $M = A + \frac{\Sigma fx'}{N} \times i$

where A stands for assumed mean, *i* for class interval, *f* for the respective frequency of the mid-value, N for the total frequency and x' for $\frac{X - A}{i}$ (the quotient obtained after division of the difference between the mid-value of the class and assumed mean by *i*).

The use of this formula can be easily understood through the following illustration:

Let us assumed Mean (A) = 42

Scores	*f*	*X*	$x' = \frac{X - A}{i}$	*fx*
65—69	1	67	5	5
60—64	3	62	4	12
55—59	4	57	3	12
50—54	7	52	2	14
45—49	9	47	1	9
40—44	11	42	0	0
35—39	8	37	–1	–8
30—34	4	32	–2	–8
25—29	2	27	–3	–6
20—24	1	22	–4	–4
				$\Sigma fx' = 26$

$$M = A + \frac{\Sigma fx'}{N} \times i = 42 + \frac{26}{50} \times 5 = 42 + 2.6 = 44.6$$

Median (M_d)

If the items of a series are arranged in ascending or descending order of magnitude, the measure or value or the central item in the series is termed the median. In this way as Bloomers and Lindquist define:

> *"The Median of a distribution is the point on the score scales below which one-half or 50 per cent of the scores fall."*

Thus, median is the score or value of the central item which divides the series into two equal parts. In this connection it should be clearly understood that central item itself is not the median. It is only the measure or value of the central item that is known as median. For example, if we arrange in ascending or descending order the marks of 5 students, then the marks obtained by 3rd student from either side will be termed as the median of the scores of the group of students under consideration.

Computation in the Case of Ungrouped Data.

There may arise two situations:

(i) When N (the number of items in series) is odd. In the case where *N i.e.* number of students in the above example, is odd (not divisible by 2) then the median can be computed by the formula

M_d= The measure or value of the $\left(\frac{N+1}{2}\right)$th item.

Example. Let the scores obtained by 7 students in an Achievement Test be 17, 47, 15, 35, 25, 39, 44. Then first of all, for calculating median we have to arrange the scores in ascending or descending order like 15, 17, 25, 35, 39, 44, 47. Here N (= 7) is odd and therefore the score of the $\left(\frac{N+1}{2}\right)$th or 4th student, *i.e.* 35 is the median of given scores.

(ii) Where N (the number of items in a series) is even— In the case where N is even (divisible by 2), then the median is determined by this following formula —

$$M_d = \frac{\text{The value of (N/2)th and (N/2+1)th item}}{2}$$

Example—Let there be a group of 8 students, whose scores are 17, 47, 15, 35, 39, 50, 29, 44.

For calculating the median of these scores we will proceed as under: The score of the (N/2)th = 35 *i.e.* 4th student

The score of the (N/2 +l)th = 39 *i.e.* 5th student

$$\text{Then Median} = \frac{35+39}{2} = 37$$

Computation of Median in case of Grouped Data (data in the form of a frequency distribution)

If the data is available in the form of a frequency distribution like the following:

Scores	*f*
65—69	1
60—64	3
55—59	4
50—54	7
45—49	9
40—44	11
35—39	8
30—34	4
25—29	2
20—24	1
	N = 50

Then calculating of median, first requires the location of median class. Actually as defined earlier, median is the measure or score of the central item.

Therefore it is needed, which is the central item whose measure we aim to determine. It is done through the formula given above in the case of ungrouped data depending upon the odd and even nature of total frequencies (N). Here in the present distribution N (= 50) is even, therefore, median will fall somewhere between the scores of 25th and 26th items in the given distribution. In the present example if we add frequencies from the above or below we can know that the class interval designated as 40—44 can be labelled as the class where the score representing median lies.

After estimating the median class the median of the distribution can be interpolated from the following formula:

$$M_d = L + \frac{N/2 - F}{f} \times i$$

Where L = Exact lower limit of the median class
F = Total of all the frequencies before the median class
F = Frequency of the median class
i = Class interval
N = Total of all the frequencies.

By applying the above formula we can compute the median of the given distribution in the following way:

$$M_d = 39.5 + \left(\frac{50/2}{11}\right) \times 5 = 39.5 + \frac{10}{11} \times 5$$

$$= 39.5 + \frac{50}{11} = 39.5 + 4.55 = 44.05$$

Some Special Situations in the Computation of Median

(a) Scores	*f*	*(b)* Scores	*f*	*(c)* Scores	*f*
55–59	5	45–49	2	20–21	2
50–54	3	40–44	5	18–19	1
45–49	8	35–39	6	16–17	0
40–44	18	30–34	0	14–15	0
35–39	15	25–29	8	12–13	2
30–34	10	20–24	3	10–11	0
25–29	7	15–19	2	8–9	0
20–24	2			6–7	2
				4–5	1
				2–3	1
				0–1	1
	N = 68		**N = 26**		**N = 10**

Let us think about the medians of the above distributions.

(a) We know by definition that median is the point on the score scale below and above which 50% cases lie. Observing through this definition the score representing median should be a common score falling between the class 35-39 and 40-44. This score is nothing but the upper limit of the class 35-39 which is also the lower limit of the class 40-44. Therefore, in this case median is 39.5.

(b) In the 2nd distribution, if we try to add the frequencies from below we see that upto class interval 25–29, 13 cases lie and by adding frequencies from above we also find that upto the class interval 35–39, 13 cases lie. In this way, the class interval 30-34 divides the distribution into two equal parts below and above which 50% cases lie. It leads us to conclude that median should be the mid-point of the class interval 30-34 and therefore 32 is the median of this distribution.

(c) In the 3rd case if we add the frequencies from below we find that upto the class interval 6–7, 5 cases lie and by adding the frequencies from above. We also find that upto the class 12–13, 5 cases lie. The median should fall in the mid-way between the two classes 8–9, and 10–11. It should be the common score represented by both these classes. This score is nothing but the upper limit of the class 8-9 and lower limit of the class 10–11 and therefore, it should be 9.5.

Mode (M_0)

Mode is defined to be the size of the variable (say a score) which occurs most frequently. It is the point on the score scale that corresponds to the maximum frequency of the distribution. In any series it is the value of the item, which is most characteristic or common and is usually repeated maximum number of items.

Computation of Mode

(a) In the case of ungrouped data

In the case of ungrouped data mode can be easily computed merely by looking at it. All that one has to do is to find out the score which is repeated maximum number of times.

Example: Suppose we have to find out the value of the mode from the following scores of the students: 25, 29, 24, 27, 28, 25, 29.

Here the score 25 is repeated maximum number of times and thus value of the mode in this case is 25.

(b) In the case of grouped data

In the case where data is available in the form of a frequency distribution, the mode Mode (M_0) = $3M_d$—2M where M_d is the median and M, the mean of the given distribution of all mean as well as median of the distribution are computed and then with the help of the above formula Mode is calculated. For illustration we can take the distribution previously given in the Table 5.2. We know the mean and median of this distribution. Now we can use these results for the computation of the mode.

$$M_d = 44.05, \quad M = 44.6$$

Therefore, $$M_o = 3 \times 44.05 - 2 \times 44.6$$
$$= 132.15 - 89.2 = 42.95$$

When to use the Mean, Median and Mode

Computation of any of the three—mean, median and mode—provides a measure of central tendency. Now which of them should be computed for a particular distribution is a question that can be raised quite often. Below we pay attention over this aspect in light of the characteristics and nature of all these measures.

(a) When to use the Mean

(i) Mean is the most reliable accurate measure of the central tendency of a distribution in comparison to median and mode. It has the greatest stability as there are less fluctuations in the means of the samples drawn from the same population. Therefore, in the case where a reliable and accurate measure of central tendency is needed, we compute mean for the given data.

(ii) Mean can be given an algebraic treatment and is better suited to further arithmetical computation. Therefore, it can be easily employed for the computation of various statistics like Standard Deviation, Coefficient of correlation, etc. Hence, when we need to know such statistics, mean is computed for the given data.

(iii) In computation of the mean we give equal weightage to every item in the series. Therefore, it is affected by the value of each item in that series. Sometimes, there are extreme items which seriously affect the position of the mean. Therefore, it is not proper to compute mean for the series that have extreme items. It should be calculated only when the series has no extreme items and each score carries equal weight in determining the central tendency.

(b) When to use the Median

(i) Median is the exact mid-point of a series as 50% cases lie below and above it. Therefore, when the exact mid-point of the distribution is desired, median is to be computed.

(ii) Median is not affected by the extreme scores in the series. Therefore, when a series contains extreme scores, the median is perhaps the most representative central measure.

(iii) In case of an open end distribution (incomplete distribution "80 and above" or "20 and below" etc.) mean is impossible to be calculated.

(iv) Mean cannot be calculated graphically. But in case of median we can compute it graphically. Therefore, when we have suitable graphs like Frequency curve, Polygon etc. we should try to compute median.

(v) The median is specifically useful for the data the items of which cannot precisely be measure quantitatively e.g. qualities like health, culture, honesty, intelligence, etc.

(c) When to use the Mode

(i) In many cases crude mode can be computed by just having a look at the data. It gives the quickest, although approximate, measure of central tendency. Therefore, in cases where a quick and approximate measure of central tendency is all that is desired, we compute mode.

(ii) Mode is that value of the item which occurs most frequently or is repeated maximum number of times in a given series. Therefore, when we need to know the most often recurring score or value of the items in a series, we compute mode. On account of this characteristic mode has unique importance in the large scale manufacturing of consumption goods. In finding the sizes of the shoes and ready-made clothes which will fit most men, the manufacturer makes use of the average indicated by mode.

(iii) Mode can be computed from the histogram and other frequency curves. Therefore, when we already have a graphical representation of the distribution in the form of such figures, it is appropriate to compute mode instead of mean

Percentiles and Percentile Ranks—Computation

As we have discussed, median is the point on the score scale which divides the series into two equal parts such that 50% of the cases lie below and above it. Proceeding on the same principle, the series may be divided into hundred parts and the values of these items (scores) are known as percentiles. These value can be computed by the same procedure as adopted for computing median. Even the formula for computing percentiles is just similar to that of computing median. Below we are giving all these formulae along with the formula for computing median

$$M_d = L + \left(\frac{N/2 - F}{f}\right) \times i$$

$$\text{1st percentile or } P_1 = L + \left(\frac{N/100 - F}{f}\right) \times i$$

$$\text{50th percentile or } P_{50} = L + \left(\frac{50N/100 - F}{f}\right) \times i = L + \left(\frac{N/2 - F}{f}\right) \times i$$

75th percentile or

$$P_{75} = L + \left(\frac{75N/2 - F}{f}\right) \times i = L + \left(\frac{3N/4 - F}{f}\right) \times i$$

In all these formulae, L represents the lower limit of the class, where, approximately, the value or score of our required median or percentile lies; N stands for the total of all frequencies; F for the total of all the frequencies before this class; f for the frequency of this particular class and i for the class interval. Now we illustrate the computation of different Percentiles by taking the following distribution:

Scores	*f*
70-79	3
60-69	2
50-59	2
40-49	3
30-39	5
20-29	4
10-19	3
0-9	2
	N = 24

(i) 10th Percentile (P_{10})

Formula, $P_{10} = L + \left(\dfrac{N/10 - F}{f}\right) \times i$

Here $\dfrac{N}{10} = \dfrac{24}{10} = 2.4.$

It is easy to locate the P_{10} lying in the interval 10–19.

Thus $P_{10} = 9.5 + \left(\dfrac{2.4-2}{3}\right) \times 10 = 9.5 + \dfrac{4}{3} = 9.5 + 1.33 = 10.83$

(ii) 25th Percentile (P_{25})

Formula $P_{25} = L + \left(\dfrac{25N/100 - F}{f}\right) \times i$

$$= 19.5 + \frac{\left(\dfrac{25 \times 24}{100} - 5\right)}{4} \times 10 = 19.5 + \frac{5}{2} = 22.$$

(iii) 60th Percentile (P_{60})

$$\text{Formula } P_{60} = L + \frac{\left(\dfrac{60N}{100} - F\right)}{f} \times i$$

Here 60th per cent of 24 $= \dfrac{60 \times 24}{100} = \dfrac{72}{5} = 14.4$

Adding the frequencies from below we see that upto the upper limit of the class 30 – 39, 14 cases lie. Therefore 60th percentile of the distribution should fall in the interval 40 – 49.

Hence $P_{60} = 39.5 + \left(\frac{14.4-14}{3}\right) \times 10 = 39.5 + 4/3 = 39.5 + 1.33 = 40.83.$

Computation of Percentile Rank

Before understanding the mechanism of computing percentile ranks from the raw scores of a group of students on such achievement/performance test, we should try to understand the difference between percentiles and percentile rank.

What are percentiles and percentile rank?

As matter of definition, a percentile may be known as a point on the distribution or score scale below which a given per cent of the cases lies. Defined in this way, the 1st percentile (written as P_1) will mean "a score point in the given series or distribution below which 1 per cent cases lie and above which 99 per cent cases lie." Similarly, the 70th percentile (P_{70}) will reveal a score point in a given series or distribution below which the scores of 70 per cent and above which 30 per cent members of the group fall.

As a matter of definition, the term percentile rank may be defined as the number representing the percentages of the total number of cases falling below the given score in a particular distribution. In such a sense, a percentile rank gives a person's relative position or the percentage of individuals' scores falling below his obtained score. For example, let us assume that Ramesh has obtained a raw score of 65 on a Mathematics test. If 80 per cent of the scores in the distribution fall below a score of 65, the percentile rank of the score of 65 is 80 and the 80th percentile is a score of 65. Thus, 65 is the point below which 80 per cent of the scores in the distribution falls. (You may conclude that percentile ranks and percentiles are just opposite to each other.)

In the light of the above clarification about the concept of percentile and percentile rank, we may form an opinion about the way of converting a raw score into a percentile rank/norm in the following manner:

1. Take the raw score (obtained on a test) that you need to get converted into a percentile rank or norm. Let it be 25.
2. Calculate the percentages of the subjects (belonging to a standardized sample) whose scores lie below the score 25. Let it be 30 per cent.
3. Then 30 will be regarded as the percentile rank or norm of the raw score of 25.

A Few important clarifications about the concept of percentiles and percentile ranks

1. Percentile ranks or norms can also be regarded as ranks in a group of 100, except that in ranking it is customary to start counting at the top, the best person in the group receiving a rank of one. With percentiles, on the other hand, we begin counting at the bottom, so that the lower the percentile, the poorer the individual's standing. (Anastasi, 1968:49)

2. These should not be confused with our well-known percentage scores. It must be remembered that where percentiles are derived scores, expressed in terms of the percentages of the persons failing below a given score belonging to a particular distribution, the percentage scores are raw scores, expressed in terms of the correct items.
3. In explaining a norm percentile rank of 95 earned by a student in the CBSE examination of national level, it may be said that he has obtained a score higher than 95 per cent of the students appearing in the examination.
4. A raw score higher than any score in the standardization sample would have a percentile rank of 100 (P_{100}), while that lower than any obtained in the standardized sample would have a percentile rank of zero (P_0). These percentiles, however, should not be confused in any case with a perfect raw score and a zero raw score.

How to compute percentile norms with a given distribution

Table 6.1: Frequency distribution of the scores earned by the subjects in a given test

Scores	*f*
70-79	3
60-69	2
50-59	2
40-49	3
30-39	5
20-29	4
10-19	3
0-9	2
	N = 24

Method 1: Involving the use of a generalized formula

The percentile rank or norm of a given raw score of a distribution (organized in a frequency table) may be easily computed by employing the following formula:

$$PR = 100/N\{F + [(X-L)/i] \times f\}$$

Where PR = Percentile rank for the desired score X

F = Cumulative frequency below the interval containing score X

X = Score for which we want the percentile rank

L = Actual lower limit of the interval containing X

i = Size of the class interval

F = Frequency of the interval containing X

N = Total number of the cases in the given frequency distribution.

Let us use this formula to compute the percentile rank of the score 22 belonging distribution given in Table 6.1

Percentile rank of the score 22:

PR = 100/24 (5 + 22 – 19.5/10 × 4) = 100/24 (5 + 2.5 × 4/10)
= 100×6/24 = 25

Method 2: Use of Cumulative Frequency Curve or Ogive

Percentile points and percentile ranks both may be read with a high degree of accuracy from an ogive (a cumulative percentage frequency graph) accurately constructed on a graph sheet. Most of the test manuals contain ogive (showing the cumulative percentage of cases falling below each score) for the easy computation and interpretation of percentile norms.

For the purpose of illustration we are here producing a smoothed ogive. See Figure 6.1.

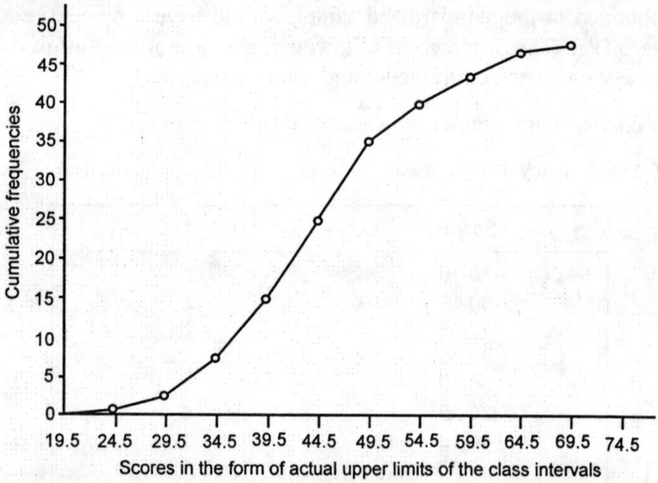

Fig. 6.1: Computation of percentile ranks or norms from an ogive.

How to Read the Percentile Rank or Norm from the Ogive

For reading the percentile rank or norm of a given score lying on the X-axis, one can proceed as under

1. Draw perpendicular lines from the points (where the given raw, scores are lying on the X-axis) extending to the ogive curve. Here in Figure 6.1, two such perpendicular lines have been drawn for the scores 39.5 and 53 lying on the X-axis.
2. Draw horizontal lines from the points where the perpendiculars intersect the ogive on the Y-axis (showing cumulative percentage frequencies).
3. You will get the points on the Y-axis indicating the corresponding percentile ranks or norms of the given raw scores.
4. In Figure 6.1 now you may see that a raw score of 39.5 has a percentile rank of 30 and a score of 53.00 has a percentile rank of 80.

7

Measures of Variability or Dispersion

Need of the Measures of Variability or Dispersion

Measures of central tendency — mean, median and mode — provide central value or typical representative of a set of scores as a whole. Through these measures we can represent a characteristic or quality of the whole group by a single number. By comparing such typical representative of the different sets of scores we can compare the achievement of the two groups. But these representative numbers give us merely an idea of the general achievement of the group as a whole, and does not show how the individual scores are spread out. Therefore, through measures of central tendency we are unable to know much about the distribution of scores in a series or characteristics of items in a group. Hence, measures of central tendency provide insufficient base for the comparison of two or more frequency distributions or sets of scores. It can be made more clear from the following example:

Let there be two small groups of boys and girls whose scores in an achievement test are such as the following:

Test Scores of Group A (boys) — 40, 38, 36, 17, 20, 19, 18, 3, 5, 4

Test Scores of Group B (girls) — 19, 20, 22, 18, 21, 23, 17, 20, 22, 18

Now the value of the Mean in both the cases is 20 and thus, so far as the mean goes, there is no difference in the performance of the two groups. Now the question arises, can we take both sets of scores as identical? Definitely there is a lot of difference between the performance of two groups. Whereas the test scores of group A are found to range from 3 to 40, the scores in group B range from 18 to 23. First group is composed of individuals who have wide individual differences. It contains either very capable or very poor individuals. The second group, on the other hand, is composed of average individuals. Individuals in this latter group are less variable than those of the former. Looking in this way, there is a great need of paying consideration to the variability or dispersion of the scores in the sets of scores or series if we want to describe and compare them.

Different Measures of Variability or Dispersion

There are chiefly, four measures of indicating variability or dispersion within the set of scores. They are:

(a) The Range (R)

(b) The Quartile Deviation (Q)
(c) The Average Deviation (*AD*)
(d) The Standard Deviation (*SD*)

Each of the above measures of variability gives us the degree of variability or dispersion by the use of a single number and tells us how the individual scores are scattered or spread over throughout the distribution or gives data.

In the following pages we will discuss these measures in brief.

Range (R)

Range is the simplest measure of variability or dispersion. It is calculated by subtracting the lowest scores in the series from the highest. But it is very rough measure of the variability of a series. It takes only extreme scores into consideration and tells nothing about the variation of the individual items.

Quartile Deviation (Q)

It is computed by the formula $Q = (Q_3 - Q_1)/2$, where Q_1 and Q_3 represent the 1st and 3rd Quartiles of the distribution under consideration. The amount Q_3 and Q_1 is nothing but the difference or range between 3rd and 1st Quartile. It is designated as the inter quartile range. For computing Quartile Deviation, this interquartile range is divided by 2 and therefore, Quartile Deviation is also named as semi-interquartile range. In this way for computing Q, the values of Q_1 and Q_3 are first determined and then by applying the above formula we try to get the value of Quartile Deviation.

Average Deviation (AD)

"Average Deviation or AD" as Garrett defines it, "is the mean of the deviation of all the separate scores in the series taken from their mean (occasionally from the median or mode.)" (1971, p. 481)

It is the simplest measure of variability that takes into account the fluctuation or variation of all the items in a series.

(i) Computation of Average Deviation (AD) from Ungrouped Data.

In the case of ungrouped data AD is calculated by the formula:

$$AD = \frac{\Sigma |x|}{N}$$

where $|x| = X - M$ = Deviation of the score from the mean of the series and $|x|$ signifies that in the deviation values we ignore the algebraic signs +ve and –ve.

The use of this formula can be explained through the following example.

Problem. Find out the Average Deviation of the scores 15, 10, 6, 8, 11 of a series.

Solution. The mean of the given series = 15 + 10 + 6 + 8 + 11 = 10

Scores X	*Deviation from the Mean* $(X - M) = x$	$\|x\|$
15	5	5
10	0	0
6	–4	4
8	–2	2
11	1	1
N = 5		$\Sigma\|x\| = 12$

By applying the formula $AD = \frac{\Sigma|x|}{N} = \frac{12}{5} = 2.4$

(ii) *Computation of Average Deviation from Grouped Data*

From grouped data *A.D.* can be computed by the formula

$$A.D. = \frac{\Sigma|fx|}{N}$$

Use of this formula can be understood through the following illustration:

Scores	*f*	*Mid-Point X*	*fx*	$x = X - M$	*fx*	$\|fx\|$
110—114	4	112	448	11.94	44.76	44.76
105—109	4	107	428	6.94	27.76	27.76
100—104	3	102	306	1.94	5.82	5.82
95—99	0	97	0	–3.06	0	0
90—94	3	92	276	–8.08	–24.18	24.18
85—89	3	87	261	–13.06	–39.18	39.18
80—84	1	82	82	–18.06	–18.06	18.06
	N = 18		Σfx = 1801			162.67 $\Sigma\|fx\|$

First of all Mean is computed.

$$\text{Here Mean} = \frac{\Sigma fx}{N} = \frac{1801}{18} = 100.06$$

Then we calculate the values of *x* by subtracting Mean from the respective values of *X* and enter them into *V* column. By multiplying these values by the respective class frequencies and ignoring the algebraic sign we get the value of $\Sigma|fx|$. Afterwards we apply the formula as below:

$$\text{AD} = \frac{\Sigma|fx|}{N} = \frac{162.76}{18} = 9.04$$

Standard Deviation (SD)

Standard Deviation of a set of scores is defined as the square root of the average of the squares of the deviations of each score from the mean.

Symbolically we can say that $SD \sqrt{\frac{\Sigma(X-M)^2}{N}} = \sqrt{\frac{\Sigma x^2}{N}}$ where X stands for individual score, *M* for mean of the given set of scores, *N* for total number of the scores and x for the deviation of each score from the mean.

Standard Deviation is regarded as a most stable and reliable measure of variability as it employs mean for its computation. It is often called as Root-mean square deviation and is denoted by the Greek letter sigma.

(a) *Computation of Standard Deviation (SD) from Ungrouped Data*: *SD* can be computed from the ungrouped scores by the following formula

$$\sigma = \sqrt{\frac{\Sigma x^2}{N}}$$

Below we illustrate the use of this formula by taking a particular example.

Problem: Calculate *SD* for the following set of test scores: 52, 50, 56, 68, 65, 62, 57, 70.

Solution. Mean of the given scores = 480/8 = 60

Scores X	*Deviation from the mean (X–M) or x*	*Squares of the Deviations x^2*	
52	–8	64	
50	–10	100	Now $\sigma = \sqrt{\frac{\Sigma x^2}{N}}$
56	–4	16	
68	8	64	
65	5	25	$= \sqrt{\frac{382}{8}}$
62	2	4	
57	–3	9	
70	10	100	$= \sqrt{47.75}$
		$\Sigma x^2 = 382$	$= 6.91$

***(b) Computation of Standard Deviation from Grouped Data*:** S.D. in case of grouped data can be computed by formula

$$S = \sqrt{\frac{\Sigma fx^2}{N}}$$

The use of the formula can be understood through the solution of the following example.

Problem: Compute SD for the frequency distribution given below on the extreme left. The mean of this distribution is 115.

I.Q. Scores	*f*	*X*	*M*	*x*	x^2	fx^2
127—129	1	128	115	13	169	169
124—126	2	125	115	10	100	200
121—123	3	122	115	7	49	147
118—120	1	119	115	4	16	16

I.Q. Scores	*f*	*X*	*M*	*x*	x^2	fx^2
115—117	6	116	115	1	1	6
112—114	4	113	115	−2	4	16
109—111	3	110	115	−5	25	75
106—108	2	107	115	−8	64	128
103—105	1	114	115	−11	121	121
100—102	1	101	115	−14	196	196
	N = 24					Σfx^2 =1074

Now $$\sigma = \sqrt{\frac{\Sigma x^2}{N}} = \sqrt{\frac{1074}{24}} = \sqrt{44.75} = 6.69$$

In the above computation work we have made use of M, the mean of the distribution. If not given in the problem, it can be computed in the following way:

Calculation of Mean — Let Assumed Mean be 116

Scores	*f*	*X (Mid- Value)*	$x' = \frac{x-A}{i}$	fx'
127—129	1	128	4	4
124—126	2	125	3	6
121—123	3	122	2	6
118—120	1	119	1	1
115—117	6	116	0	0
112—114	4	113	-1	-4
109—111	3	110	-2	-6
106—108	2	107	-3	-6
103—105	1	104	-4	-4
100—102	1	101	-5	-5
	N = 24			$fx' = -8$

Formula $$M = A + \frac{\Sigma fx'}{N} \times i$$

$$= 116 - \frac{8}{24} \times 3 = 116 - 1 = 115$$

Mean = 115.

(c) *Computation of Standard Deviation from Grouped Data by Short-cut Method*: SD from grouped data can also be computed by the following formula:

$$\sigma = i\sqrt{\frac{\Sigma fx'^2}{N} - \left(\frac{\Sigma fx'}{N}\right)^2}$$

Where the notation have the same meaning as desired earlier. The use of this formula can be explained by solving the problem given under the case (b).

I.Q. Scores	f	X	$x' = \frac{x - A}{i}$	fx'	fx'^2
127—129	1	128	4	4	16
124—126	2	125	3	6	18
121—123	3	122	2	6	12
118—120	1	119	1	1	1
115—117	6	116	0	0	0
112—114	4	113	–1	–4	4
109—111	3	110	–2	–6	12
106—108	2	107	–3	–6	18
103—105	1	104	–4	–4	16
100—102	1	101	–5	–5	25
	N = 24			$\sum fx' = -8$	$\sum fx^2 = 122$

$$\text{Formula } \sigma = i\sqrt{\frac{\sum fx'^2}{N} - \left(\frac{\sum fx'}{N}\right)^2}$$

$$= 3\sqrt{\frac{122}{24} - \left(\frac{-8}{24}\right)^2}$$

$$= 3\sqrt{\frac{122}{24} = \frac{64}{24 \times 24}}$$

$$= \frac{3}{24}\sqrt{122 \times 24 - 64}$$

$$= \frac{1}{8}\sqrt{2864} = \frac{53.51}{8}$$

Standard Deviation = 6.69

8
Correlation

Introduction

In Education as well as Psychology there are times when it is needed to know whether there exists any relationship between the different abilities of the individual or they are independent of each other. Consequently, there are numerous questions like the following which have to be answered:

(i) Does scholastic achievement depend upon the general intelligence of a child?

(ii) Is it true that the height of the children increases with the increase in their age?

(iii) Is there any relationship between the size of the skull and general intelligence of the individuals?

(iv) Is it true that Dull children tend to be more neurotic than the bright children?

The questions and problems like the above in which there is a need of finding out the relationship between two variables (Age and height, Intelligence and Achievement etc.) can be tackled properly by the method of correlation.

There are many types of correlation like Linear, Curvilinear, Biserial, Partial or Multiple correlation that are computed in statistics. As we, in this text, aim to have an elementary knowledge of the statistical methods we will take only the Linear correlation in the following pages.

Linear Correlation

This is the simplest kind of correlation to be found between the two sets of scores or variables. Actually, when the relationship between two sets of scores or variables can be represented graphically by a straight line, it is known as Linear Correlation. Such type of correlation clearly reveals how the change in one variable is accompanied by a change in the other or to what extent increase or decrease in one is accompanied by the increase or decrease in other.

The correlation between two sets of measures of variables can be positive or negative. It is said to be positive when an increase (or decrease) in one corresponds to an increase (or decrease) in the other. It is negative when increase corresponds to decrease and decrease to increase. There is also possibility of third type of correlation *i.e.* zero correlation between the two sets of measures or variables if there exists no relationship between them.

Coefficient of Correlation

For expressing the degree of relationship quantitatively between two sets of measures of variables we usually take the help of an index that is known as coefficient of correlation. It is a kind of ratio which expresses the extent to which changes in one variable are accompanied changes in the other variable. It involves no units and varies from -1 (indicating perfect negative correlation) to +1 (indicating perfect positive correlation). In case the coefficient of correlation is zero, it indicates zero correlation between two set of measures.

Computation of Coefficient of Correlation

There arc two different methods of computing coefficient of correlation (linear). These are:

(A) Rank Difference Method

(B) Product Moment Method.

Below we discuss them one by one.

(A) Rank difference Method of Computing Coefficient of Correlation

In computing coefficient of correlation between two sets of scores achieved by the individuals, with the help of this method we require ranks *i.e.* positions of merits of these individuals in the possession of certain characteristics. The coefficient of correlation computed by this method, as it considers only the ranks of the individuals in the characteristics A and B is known as Rank correlation co-efficient and is designated by Greek letter (Rho). Sometimes it is also known as Spearman's coefficient of correlation after the name of its inventor.

In case where we do not have scores and have to work with data in which differences between the individuals in the possession of certain characteristics can be expressed only by ranks. Rank correlation coefficient is the only correlation coefficient that can be computed. But this does not mean that it cannot be computed from the usual data given in scores. In case the data contain scores of individuals, we can compute by converting them into ranks. For example, if the marks of a group of 5 students are given as 17, 25, 9, 35, 18 we will rank them as 4, 2, 5, 1 and 3. We determine the rank of position of the individuals in both the given sets of scores. These ranks are then subjected to further calculation for the determination of the coefficient of correlation.

How it is done can be understood properly through the following illustration:

Example: 1

Individual	*Marks in the Subject of History X*	*Marks in the Subject of Civics Y*	*Rank in History R_2*	*Rank in Civics R_2*	*Difference in Rank irrespective of signs +ive of -ive $\|d\|$ $\|R_1–R_2\|$*	*Difference squared d^2*
A	80	82	2	3	1	1
B	45	86	11	2	9	81
C	55	50	10	10	0	0
D	56	48	9	11	2	4
E	58	60	8	9	1	1
F	60	62	7	8	1	1
G	65	64	6	7	1	1
H	68	65	5	6	1	1
I	70	70	4	5	1	1
J	75	74	3	4	1	1
K	85	90	1	1	0	0
	N = 11					$\sum d^2 = 92$

$$\text{Formula } \rho = 1 - \frac{6\sum d^2}{N\left(N^2-1\right)} = 1 - \frac{6\times 92}{11\left(11^2-1\right)} = 1 - \frac{6\times 92}{11\times 120}$$

$$= 1 - \frac{23}{55} = 1 - .42 = .58$$

Example: 2

Individuals	*Scores in Test X*	*Scores in Test Y*	*Rank in X_1, R_1*	*Rank in X_2, R_2*	$\|R_1 - R_2\|$ $=\|d\|$	d^2
A	12	21	8	6	2	4
B	15	25	6.5	3.5	3	9
C	24	35	2	2	0	0
D	20	24	4	5	1	1
E	8	16	10	9	1	1
F	15	18	6.5	7	0.5	0.25
G	20	25	4	3.5	0.5	0.25
H	20	16	4	9	5	25
I	11	16	9	9	0	0
J	26	38	1	1	0	0
N= 10						$\sum d^2 = 40.5$

Now $$\rho = 1 - \frac{6\sum d^2}{N(N^2-1)}$$

$$= 1 - \frac{6 \times 40.5}{10(10^2-1)} = 1 - \frac{6 \times 40.5}{10 \times 99}$$

$$= 1 - \frac{8.1}{33}$$

$$= 1 - .245$$

$$= 0.755$$

Steps for the Calculation of ρ

1. First of all it is required to assign position of merit or rank to each individual on either test. These ranks are put under column 3 (designated as R_1) and 4 (designated as R_2), respectively. The task of assigning ranks in the cases like example 1st is not difficult. But in the cases, like example 2nd, where two or more individuals are found to achieve same score, some difficulty arises. In the above example, in the first test X, B and F are two individuals who have the same score *i.e.* 15. Therefore, score 15 occupies 6th position in order of merit. But now the question arises which one of the two individuals B and F should be ranked as 6th or 7th. In order to overcome this difficulty we equally share the rank 6th and 7th between them and thus rank each one of them as 6.5.

Similarly, if there are three persons who have the same score and share the same ranks, we take the average of the ranks claimed by these persons. For example, we can take the score 20 in the 2nd example which is shared by three individuals D, G and H. It is ranked third in the whole series and therefore the ranks 3, 4 and 5 are shared equally by D, G and H, and hence we attribute rank 4 to each of them.

2. After writing down the allotted ranks to all the individuals on either of the two tests, the differences in these ranks are calculated. In doing so we do not consider the algebraic signs +ive or -ive of the difference. This difference is written under column 5th (designated as $|d|$).

3. In the next column (designated as d^2) we square up the Rank difference or the values of d written in the column 5th.

4. Now we calculate the total of all the values of d^2 and this sum is designated as Σd^2.

5. Now the value of ρ is calculated by the formula $\rho = 1 - \frac{6\sum d^2}{N(N^2-1)}$

where d^2 stands for the sum of the squares of differences between the ranks of the scores on two different tests and N for the number of individuals whose scores are under consideration for computing.

(B) Product Moment Method of Computing Coefficient of Correlation

This method is also known as Pearson Product Moment method in the honour of the English statesman Karl Pearson who is said to be the inventor of this method. The coefficient of correlation computed by this method is known as Product Moment coefficient of correlation and symbolically represented by '*r*'

(a) The calculation of 'r' from Ungrouped Data.

The basic formula for the computation of 'r' for the ungrouped data by this method is

$$r = \frac{\Sigma xy}{\sqrt{\Sigma x^2, \Sigma y^2}}$$

where x and *y* represent the deviation of scores in the tests X and Y from the means of each distribution.

The procedure of calculating *r* by this formula can be understood by the following illustration:

Indivi-duals	*Scores in Text X*	*Scores in Text Y*	*x (X–Mx)*	*y (Y–My)*	*Σxy*	*x^2*	*y^2*
A	15	60	–10	10	–100	100	100
B	25	70	0	20	0	0	400
C	20	40	–5	–10	50	25	100
D	30	50	5	0	0	25	0
E	35	30	–10	–20	–200	100	400
					$\Sigma xy = -250$	$\Sigma x^2 = 250$	$\Sigma y^2 = 1000$

Mean of series X (Mx) = 25
Mean of series Y (My) = 50

Formula $$r = \frac{\Sigma xy}{\sqrt{\Sigma x^2, \Sigma y^2}} = \frac{-250}{\sqrt{250 \times 1000}} = \frac{-250}{\sqrt{250000}}$$

$$R = \frac{-25}{500} = -\frac{1}{2} = -0.5$$

(b) *Computation of r directly from raw scores when deviations are taken from zero* (without calculating deviations from the means). Here we apply the formula.

$$r = \frac{N\Sigma XY - \Sigma X.\Sigma Y}{\sqrt{\left[N\Sigma X^2 - (\Sigma X)^2\right]\left[N\Sigma Y^2 - (\Sigma Y)^2\right]}}$$

The use of this formula can be understood through the following example:

Subject	*Scores in 1st Test (X)*	*Scores in 2nd Test (Y)*	*XY*	X^2	Y^2
A	5	12	60	25	144
B	3	15	45	9	225
C	2	11	22	4	121
D	8	10	80	64	100
E	6	18	108	36	324
N = 5	ΣX = 24	ΣY = 66	ΣXY = 315	$\Sigma X^2 = 138$	$\Sigma Y^2 = 914$

$$r = \frac{5\times315-24\times66}{\sqrt{[5\times138-576][5\times914-66\times66]}}$$

$$= \frac{1575-1650}{\sqrt{[690-576][4570-4356]}}$$

$$= \frac{-75}{\sqrt{24396}} = \frac{-75}{156.2} = -0.48$$

Ans. r = –0.48

9
Normal Probability Curve (NPC)

What is Normal Distribution and Normal Probability Curve?

The literal meaning of the term normal is average. We have made use of this term in chapter 3rd of the text while computing the average or mean value from the data related to various assessment and devices like achievement tests, psychological tests, inventories and rating scales. Those who attain this mean value are termed as normal, while whose scores fall below and above this value are termed as above and below averages in terms of the quality or characteristics assessed by that test or tool.

If we try to analyse the data derived from an assessment device for a population of the students, we may notice that there lies a lot of differences among their scores. However, much of the data collected from the achievement and psychological tests and tools follow the pattern and rules of a normal distribution. Let us see what do we mean by the term normal distribution. Nature have been kind enough to distribute quite equally most of the things and attributes like height, weight, wealth, beauty, intelligence and the like among the population in a normal way. The same is also true for the distribution of the achievement and performance scores through the use of one or the other assessment tool or devices in the field of school education.

If we plot such a distribution of data (referred to as normal distribution) on a graph paper we would get an interesting typical curve often resembling a vertical cross section of a bell shown in the Fig. 9.1 below. This bell shaped curve is called a normal curve.

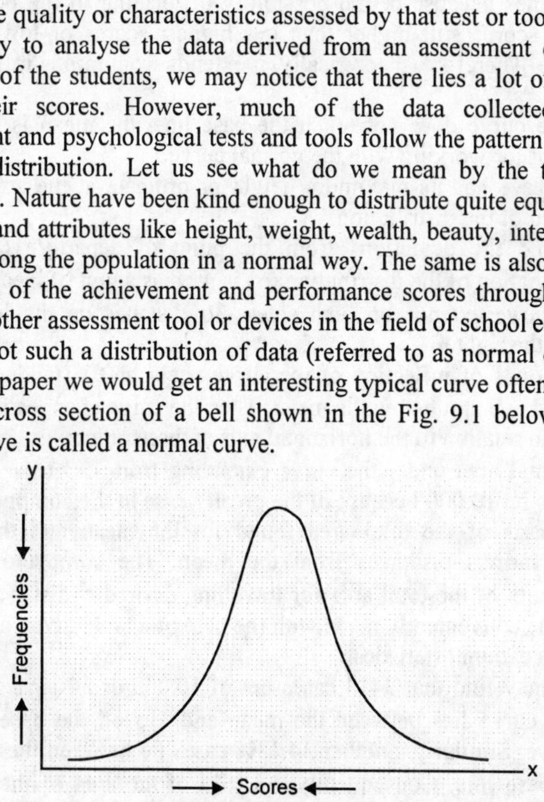

Fig. 9.1: Normal Curve

The data from a certain coin or a dice-throwing experiment involving a chance success or probability, if plotted on a graph paper, give a frequency curve which closely resembles the normal curve. It is because of this reason and because of its origin from a game of chance that the normal curve is often called the normal probability curve.

Laplace and Gauss (1777-1855) derived this curve independently. They worked on experimental errors in Physics and Astronomy and found the errors to be distributed normally. This is the reason why the curve representing the normal characteristics is also named as normal curve or error or simply the curve of error where 'error' is used in the sense of a deviation from the true value. Because of its discovery by Laplace and Gauss, the curve is also named as Gaussian curve in the honour of Gauss.

Characteristics and Properties of a Normal Curve

1. For this curve, mean, median and mode are the same.
2. The curve is perfectly symmetrical.
3. The curve is asymptotic. It approaches but never touches the base line at the extremes because of the possibility of locating in the population, a case which scores still higher than our highest scores or lower than our lowest score. Therefore, theoretically, it extends from minus infinity to plus infinity.
4. As the curve does not touch the base line, the mean is used as the starting point for working with the normal curve.
5. The curve has its maximum height or ordinate at the starting point, *i.e.,* the mean of the distribution.
6. To find the deviations from the point of departure (*i.e.,* mean), standard deviation of the distribution (σ) is used as a unit of measurement.
7. The curve extends on both sides -3σ distance on the left to + 3σ distance on the right.
8. The points of inflection of the curve occur at +1 standard deviation unit (± lσ) above and below the mean. Thus the curve changes from convex to concave in relation to the horizontal axis at these points.
9. The total area under the curve extending from -3σ to + 3σ is taken arbitrarily to be 10,000 because of the greater ease in the computation of the fractional parts of the total area found for the mean and the ordinates erected at various distances from the mean. The computation of such fractional parts of the total area for travelling desired σ distances from the mean may be conveniently made with the help of a table given in all the text books of educational statistics.
10. We may find that 3413 cases out of 10,000 or 34.13% of the entire area of the curve lies between the mean and +lσ on the base line of the normal curve. Similarly, another 34.13% cases lie between the mean and – lσ on the base line. Consequently, 68.26% of the area of the curve falls within the limits +1 Standard deviation (±lσ) unit from the mean. Going

further it may be found out that 95.44% case lie from -2σ to + 2σ and 99.74% cases lie from –3σ to + 3σ. Consequently only 26 cases in 10,000 (10,000 – 9974) should be expected to lie beyond the range ± 3σ in a large sample as shown in Fig. 9.2.

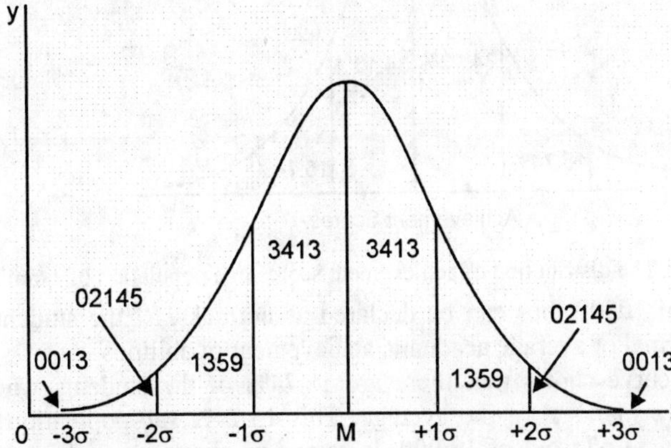

Fig. 9.2: Normal curve showing areas at different distances from the mean

An Illustration of Concept of Normal Distribution and Curve

Let us try to illustrate the concept of normal distribution and normal curve with hypothetical data related with the distribution of the achievement scores over a given population of the examines.

For having a large sample of population of the examinees let us approach the Board of School Examination of a state for the record of last year XII class annual examination. We may have the total marks scores of all the examinees appearing in the said examination arranged serially according to their roll numbers. Out of this huge data we can randomly select the total marks scores of 10,000 students for our study. Let us now calculate the average score or mean value of the sample. For this purpose, we will add individual total marks of these 10,000 students and then divide it by 10,000 for getting mean or average score value for the sample. If we try to analyse the total marks earned by this population of 10,000, we will find that majority of them have either earned the mean average score or lie quite near to this value. There are very few who have earned distinction marks or got very low marks. In case we try to plot the total marks (scores) earned by these 10,000 students on a sheet of graph paper by taking scores on x-axis and no. of students earning these scores (frequencies) on y-axis, we can have a bell-shaped curve (shown in Fig. 9.3)

Let us analysis the pattern of the distribution of achievement scores in the population of examines.

1. As revealed by this curve, we can locate the majority, 34.13% + 34.13%, *i.e.,* 68.26% of the students either getting marks equal to the mean average value or lying quite nearer to this value. This sub-population of

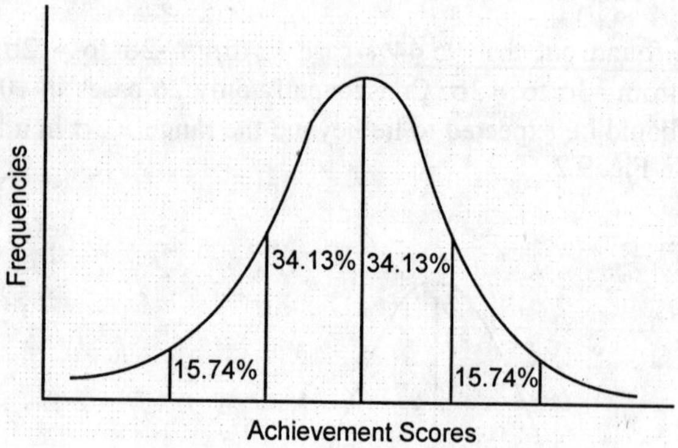

Fig. 9.3: The distribution of achievement scores in a population of examines

6826 out of 10000 thus can be declared as normal, *i.e.,* the students who possess normal or average academic achievement of abilities.

2. The curve shows that there are 15.74% of the students who have earned more marks than the average. This 15.74% sub-population of the students, *i.e.,* 1,574 out of 10,000, is named as above average in terms of their academic achievements. A similar percentage, *i.e.,* 15.74% of the students also lie on the other side of the mean value. It shows that there are 15.74% students, *i.e.,* 1574 out of 10000, who have got less marks than the average value. These students are named as below average or sub-normals in respect to their academic achievement in XII class final examination.

3. The normal curve thus can portrait the pattern of distribution of an attribute in a given population. Here it has demonstrated that out of 10,000, the majority 68.26%, *i.e.,* 6,826 out of 10000 consists of averages. There are only 15.74% *i.e.,* 1574 out of 10000 who are below average and a similar percentages 15.74%, *i.e.,* 1,574 out of 10,000 who are labelled as above average.

In the light of above findings and analysis we can easily conclude that distribution of assessment scores in a given population follows the pattern of a normal curve.

Uses and Application of Normal Probability Curve (NPC)

Normal Probability Curve (NPC) has wide significance and applications in the field of measurement concerning education. Some of its main applications are discussed in the following sections:

1. Use as a Model

Normal probability curve represents a model distribution. It can be used as a model to

(i) compare various distributions with it *i.e.,* to say, whether the distribution is normal or not and if not, in what way it diverges from the normal;

(ii) compare two or more distributions in terms of overlapping; and
(iii) evaluate students' performance from their scores.

2. Computing Percentiles and Percentile Ranks

Normal probability curve may be conveniently used for computing percentiles and percentile ranks in a given normal distribution.

3. Understanding and Applying the Concept of Standard Errors of Measurement

The normal curve as we have pointed out earlier, is also known as the normal curve of error or simply the curve of error on the grounds that it helps in understanding the concept of standard errors of measurement. For example, if we compute mean for the distributions of various samples taken from a single population, then, these means will be found to be distributed normally around the mean of the entire population. The sigma distance of a particular sample mean may help us determine the standard error of measurement for the mean of that sample.

4. Ability Grouping

A group of individuals may be conveniently grouped into certain. categories as A, B, C, D, E (Very good, good, average, poor, very poor) in terms of some trait (assumed to be normally distributed), with the help of a normal curve.

5. Transforming and Combining Qualitative Data

Under the assumption of normality of the distributed variable, the sets of qualitative data such as ratings, letter grades and categorical ranks on a scale may be conveniently transformed and combined to provide an average rating for each individual.

6. Converting Raw Scores into Comparable Standard Normalized Scores

Sometimes, we have records of an individual's performance on two or more different kinds of assessment tests and we wish to compare his score on one test with the score on the other. Unless the scales of these two tests are the same, we cannot make a direct comparison. With the help of a normal curve, we can convert the raw scores belonging to different tests into standard normalized scores like sigma (or z scores) and *T*-scores. For converting a given raw score into a z score, we subtract the mean of the scores of the distribution from the respective raw scores and divide it by the standard deviation of the distribution $\left(i.e., z = \frac{X - M}{\sigma}\right)$. In this way, a standard z score clearly indicates how many standard deviation units of a raw score is above or below the mean and thus provides a standard scale for the purpose of valuable comparison. Since, z values may carry negative signs and decimals, they are converted into T values by multiplying by some constant and added to a second constant, *i.e.*, using the formula T score = 10z +50.

7. Determine the Relative Difficulty of Test Items

Normal curve provides the simplest rational method of scaling test items for difficulty and therefore, may be conveniently employed for determining the relative difficulty of test questions, problems and other test items.

Skewness and Kurtosis

In normal curve or an approximately normal curve, as we may observe the nature of the distribution of the data always indicates that scores of majority of individuals included in the sample of a study are centered around the mean or average. However, it is not essential that in all the cases related to the research studies the distribution of the data will always lead to normal or approximately normal curves. In cases where the scores of individuals in the group seriously deviate from the average, the curves representing these distributions also deviate from the shape of a normal curve. This deviation or divergence from normality tends to vary in the following two ways:

(a) In terms of skewness and (ii) In terms of Kurtosis. Let as try to know about the concepts related to skewness and Kurtosis one by one.

Skewness

Skewness refers to the lack of symmetry. A normal curve is a perfectly symmetrical curve. In case the curve is folded along the vertical middle line (perpendicular drawn from the highest point of the curve to its base line) the two sides of the base line will overlap. Also, for this curve, mean, median and mode are the same. In many distributions which deviate from the normal, the values of mean, median and mode are different and there is no symmetry between the right and the left halves of the curve. Such distributions are said to be skewed, being inclined more toward the left or the right to the centre of the curve as shown in Figures 9.4 and 9.5. For comparison, a normal (symmetrical) curve is also provided in Figure 9.6.

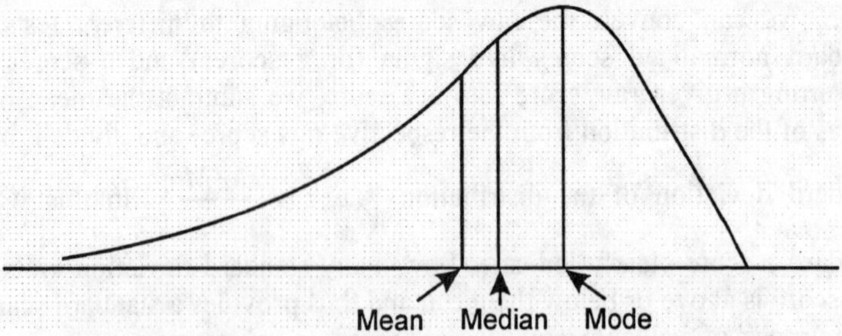

Fig. 9.4: Negative skewness (the curve inclines more to the left).

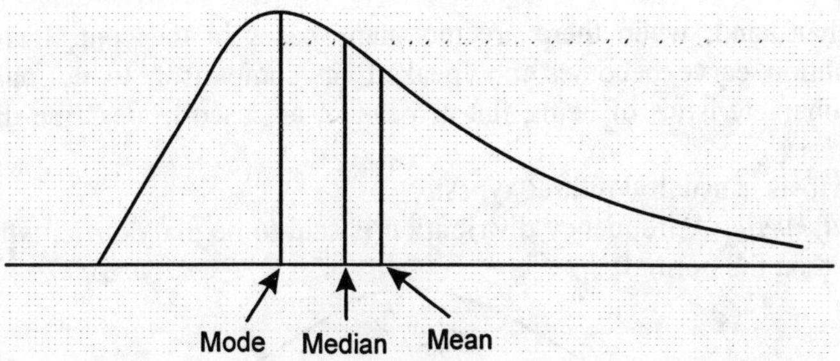

Fig. 9.5: Positive skewness (the curve inclines more to the right).

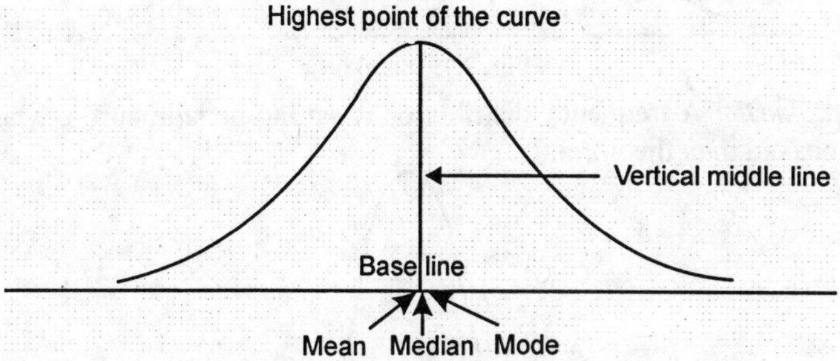

Fig. 9.6: Normal (symmetrical) curve.

As illustrated in the given figures, there are two types of skewed distributions. The distributions are said to be skewed negatively when there are many individuals in a group with their scores higher than the average score of the group. Similarly, the distributions are said to be skewed positively when there are more individuals in a group who score less than the average score for their group.

Skewness in a given distribution may be computed by the following formula:

$$\text{Skewness} = \frac{3(\text{Mean} - \text{Median})}{\text{Standard Deviation}}$$

or

$$S_k = \frac{3(M - M_d)}{SD}$$

In case when the percentiles are known, the value of skewness may be computed from the following formula:

$$S_k = \frac{P_{90} + P_{10}}{2} - P_{50}$$

Kurtosis

When there are very few individuals whose scores are near to the average score for their group (too few cases in the central area of the curve) the curve representing such a distribution becomes 'flattened' in the middle. On the other hand, when there are too many cases in the central area, the distribution curve becomes too 'peaked' in comparison to normal. Both these characteristics of being flat or peaked, are used to describe the term *kurtosis.*

Kurtosis is usually of three types:

Platykurtic: A frequency distribution is said to be platykurtic, when it is flatter than the normal.

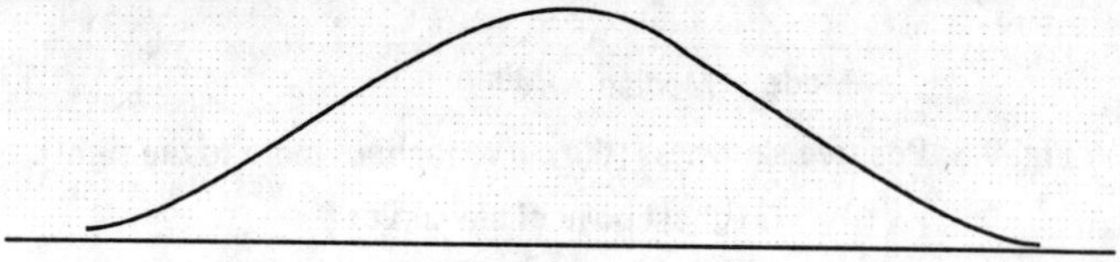

Fig. 9.7: Platykurtic

Leptokurtic: A frequency distribution is said to be laptokurtic, when it is more peaked than the normal.

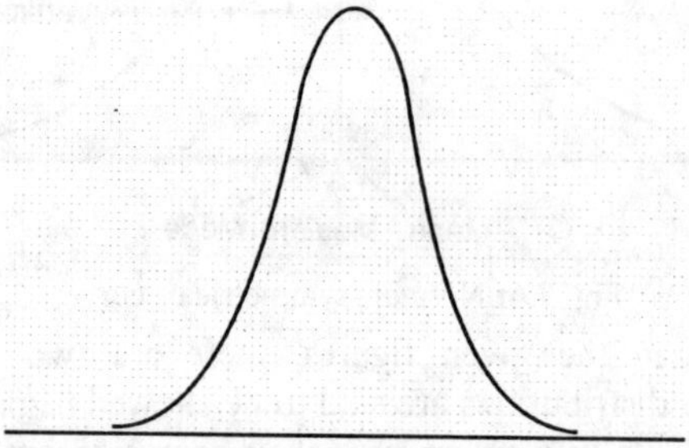

Fig 9.8: Leptokurtic

Mesokurtic: A frequency distribution is said to be mesokurtic, when it almost resembles the normal curve (neither too flattened nor too peaked).

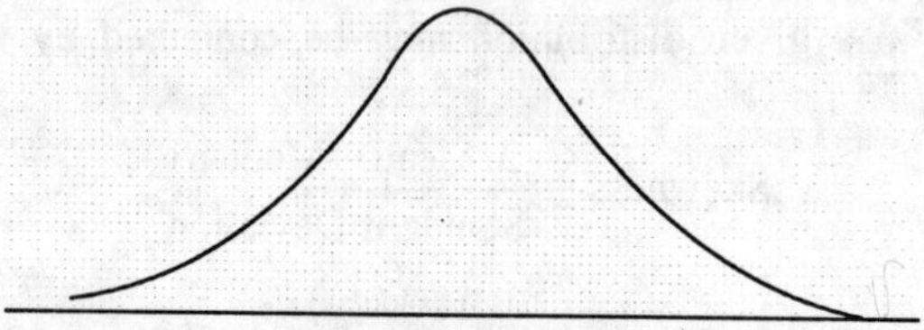

Fig. 9.9: Mesokurtic

The value of kurtosis for a given curve may be computed through the following formula:

$$\text{Kurtosis} = \frac{\text{Quartile deviation}}{\text{90th percentile} - \text{10th percentile}}$$

or

$$K_u = \frac{Q}{P_{90} - P_{10}}$$

In the case of a normal curve, this value is equal to 0.263. Consequently, if the value of kurtosis is greater than 0.263, the distribution is said to be platykurtic; if less than 0.263, the distribution is leptokurtic.

10

New Trends in Evaluation

Introduction

Assessment or evaluation as we have known and discussed in the previous chapters of this text helps us much in taking proper judgement about the learning outcomes of the students resulted through one or the other processes of teaching-learning. We make use of a variety of tools, techniques and devices for carrying out the needed assessment/evaluation of the learning outcomes of the students and then the needed task of scoring, processing, analysing and interpretation is performed for deriving necessary conclusions and getting needed feedback for bringing improvement in the processes and products of teaching-learning. The work carried out in all such aspects and dimensions of the assessment of learning outcomes needs to be quite systematic, objective and purposeful and therefore efforts are always made to bring necessary improvement in the practices employed in the field of assessment or evaluation. Various practices, policies and insights have emerged on account of a persistent struggle for bringing improvement in the system of assessment or evaluation. As a result, we may witness quite useful practices working at present in our system of the evaluation/assessment of the learning outcomes of the students besides many of them waiting for being practised in the coming future. In this chapter, here we would like to throw light on these emerging new trends in evaluation named as below:

(i) Grading system
(ii) Choice Based Credit System (CBCS)
(iii) Computer based on-line examination
(iv) Open book examination
(v) Question banks and
(vi) Examination on demand.

Let us discuss them one by one now.

Grading System

Grading system calls for providing letters grades to the students for their educational achievements instead of declaring them passed or failed or assigning numerical marks on a 100 point scale. It is preferred to the old system of percentage marking on account of the following reasons.

(i) It is simple to assign grading than the exact numerical marking involving no biases and subjectivity.

(ii) Examiners do differ in their marking on account of the subjectivity and standard of their marking. Grading reduces the subjectivity and unreliability on the part of the examiners.

(iii) In the old system, there is a provision of pass-fail or assigning divisions 1st, 2nd or 3rd for a certain percentage of marks obtained by the students. Grading makes it more wider by providing more graded categories. There is a practice in the old system of bunching the marks at the end for declaring pass or assigning particular divisions. Grading system helps in removing this evil,

(iv) Usually different subjects have different ranging marks, and combination of such heterogeneous scores as an aggregate or total marks for pass-fail or division is quite unsound and inaccurate from statistical as well as mathematical angles. Grading system provides good alternative for removing this defect.

(v) Grading system provides scaling of the evaluation on a uniform basis for better comparison and combination of the evaluation outcomes in the different subjects and by the different examiners.

Methods of Grading

Generally two types of letter grades are assigned — one is to assign A, B, C, D or E and the other consists of assigning O, A, B, C, D representing outstanding, very good, good, poor or very poor level of performances. For assigning such letter grades generally two methods known as absolute grading method and relative grading method are employed. Let us discuss these ways.

Absolute Grading Method

In such grading method a pre-determined level or standard is fixed for assigning letter grades. It can be carried out in two ways.

(i) A pre-established percentage scores required for a given grade is fixed. In other words we fix different ranges of percentage marks for assigning them grade letter like given below:

Grade	**Scores Percentage**
O	80% and above
A	70-79%
B	60-69%
C	50-59%
D	Less than 50%

(ii) Another form of the absolute grading is known as criterion-referenced grading. Here the criterion performance standard is fixed by the teacher or authorities in advance in the light of the difficulty level of the test and the standard or quality of learning performance needed from the learners. In other words, the decision is taken well before examining or testing the students that what performance (in terms of the changes in their behaviour) will help them to earn various letter grades. The performance level and letter grades can be represented as below:

Grade	Performance Level
	(in relation to the achievement of pre-determined objectives)
O	Outstanding (Excellent)
A	Above Average (Very good)
B	Average (Good)
C	Below Average (Poor)
D	Inadequate (Very Poor)

Relative Grading Method

In this method grades are provided on the basis of the comparative or relative positions (ranks) of the students in their class or group. In usual practice, relative grading follows the 'normal curve' distribution for the allocation of grades. The assumption is that in general, the distribution of marks over a population of students follows the distribution pattern of a normal curve. The area under the normal curve may be statistically divided into equal segments helping us to mark the percentage of cases falling in each segment. This further may help us to take the decision like below.

Grade	**Percentage of cases for being assigned the given grade**
O	Top 7% of a class or group
A	Top middle 24% of a class or group
B	Middle 38% of a class or group
C	Bottom middle 24% of a class or group
D	Bottom 7% of a class or group

The decision about the top 7%, the next 24%, middle 38% and so on may be taken on the basis of numeral scores earned or performance level shown by the students on any evaluation measure. The students roll numbers may then be arranged in descending order on the basis of their numerical scores or performances ratings. Top 7% are then assigned grade O, next 24% grade A, another next 38% grade B and so on.

Choice-based Credit System (CBCS)

Choice based credit system (CBCS), a practice prevalent now a days in a number of colleges and universities represents an altogether new trend and practice in the field of education and evaluation-besides other practices like Semester System, CCE and Grading systems all ready existing in the system of education-school as well as higher education. Let us see what it is and how does it operate or function.

What is the Choice-based Credit System (CBCS)?

It is one of the major evaluation-cum-academic reform movement running at present in the existing higher education system through the initiation, guidance and support of the University Grants Commission (UGC). It mainly stands for providing needed autonomy to the learners and higher education institutions with a clear cut aim of bringing qualitative improvement in the evaluation-cum-academic system for meeting the challenges of the changed times particularly in reference to globalization.

As the name suggests, choice based credit system has two major distinctive features in the name of choice and credit.

A. The term choice in this system stands for

(i) allowing the learners to make choices in terms of what to learn (choose from the prescribed courses *i.e.* subjects or papers referred as core, elective and minor or soft skill courses).

(ii) allow them to make choices in terms of learning at their own pace.

(iii) allowing them a choice or liberty to continue the studies in the existing institution or join other institution for their further studies with a facility of transferring credit earned so far to the newly joined institution/programmes.

(iv) The term choices on the part of institutions (colleges or universities) here means that they have to enjoy greater freedom and autonomy in making their choices, about what to teach, and how. The decision about the running of the type of programmes, courses etc. will be absolutely taken by them as they may consider appropriate for bringing quality in education within the framework of the National policy.

B. The term credit in this system has its connection with the management and evaluation of the teaching-learning process and its outcomes. The system recommends to provide credit scores, on the basis of what has been taught/done in the institution in forms of the teaching of one or other courses and what has been learned by the learner as revealed through the ongoing evaluation process.

What has prompted to adopt Choice Based Credit System?

The question here may emerge that what has prompted to opt for choice based credit system (CBCS) in higher education.

1. There was a greater need for replacing teacher-centered and subject centered education system with a need based learner-centered education system.

2. The information giving and rote learning was dominating the entire system of evaluation-cum-academic system of the higher education. It needed to be replaced by a need based teaching-learning system. What is learned and taught in the institutions must have its direct link with the necessities, problems and expectations of real life. The courses, programmes and activities should be so selected and executed as to help the learners in their present living and future prospectus.

3. There are great individual differences among the learners in terms of their learning potential, interests and future planning. Thus, there was a

need of a wide variety of choices available for the students to opt for their learning at their own will and interests in the college and universities in relation to the study of a particular course or going through a degree/certificate programme.

4. There is a pressure from the present generation youths on the colleges and universities in relation to address the issues like below.

- Why should not a student who is working on a part-time basis be allowed to stretch his studies in a college or university to four or five years instead of 3 years according to his convenience?
- Why should there be a kind of compulsion to complete a degree programme in three years? Can it not be adjusted according to his own potential and learning pace?
- Why is there no facility or provision to change from one college/ university to other college/university with the transfer of credits earned from the former to the transferred college/university on the national as well as international basis?
- Why there should not be a scope for collaborating with industries and employing institutions to have on the spot work experiences/ internship and earn credit scores for the same and why the same may not be included in computing the total credit for a programme/course?
- Why should not there be a change in the evaluation system in the form of continuous and comprehensive evaluation by providing weightage to their all round performances instead of the mere scholastic ones and make it a continuous and formative in its all way?
- Why should not there be a proper provision of wide choices/options for the students in going through one or other courses according to their tastes, requirements and abilities instead of being forced to go through the fixed courses/subjects for passing out a programme/obtaining degree in one or the other discipline?

In this way there were many issues and pressures on the Government of India and concerning agencies responsible for the administration and organization of higher education, and also there were a number of recommendations available in this case from the reports of the committees and commissions like National Knowledge Commission (2008-2009), Yashpal Committee (2009), that prepared a proper ground for introducing choice-based credit system in the field of higher education.

How does the Choice Based Credit System operate or function?

We can try to understand the mechanism of the operation of choice based credit system under the heads mentioned below.

A. Terminology used or key words employed.

B. Components or constituents of choice-based credit system. Let us try to discuss them one by one.

A. Terminology used or key words applied

In order to work with choice-based credit system, it is first quite essential to get acquainted with the terminology or the key words employed in its operation. UGC in its guide lines has provided the same in the following way.

1. Academic Year: Two consecutive (one odd + one even) semesters constitute one academic year.

2. Choice Based Credit System (CBCS): The CBCS provides choice for students to select from the prescribed courses (core, elective or minor or soft skill courses) and assigns credit for the course outcomes.

3. Course: Usually referred to, as 'papers' is a component of a programme. All courses need not carry the same weight. The courses should define learning objectives and learning outcomes. A course may be designed to comprise lectures/ tutorials/laboratory work/ field work/ outreach activities/ project work/ vocational training/viva/ seminars/ term papers/ assignments/ presentations/self-study, etc. or a combination of some of these.

4. Credit Based Semester System (CBSS): Under the CBSS, the requirement for awarding a degree or diploma or certificate is prescribed in terms of number of credits to be completed by the students.

5. Credit Point: It is the product of grade point and number of credits for a course.

6. Credit: A unit by which the course work is measured. It determines the number of hours of instructions required per week. One credit is equivalent to one hour of teaching (lecture or tutorial) or two hours of practical work/field work per week.

7. Cumulative Grade Point Average (CGPA): It is a measure of overall cumulative performance of a student over all semesters. The CGPA is the ratio of total credit points secured by a student in various courses in all semesters and the sum of the total credits of all courses in all the semesters. It is expressed up to two decimal places.

8. Grade Point: It is a numerical weight allotted to each letter grade on a 10-point scale.

9. Letter Grade: It is an index of the performance of students in a said course. Grades are denoted by letters O, A+, A, B+, B, C, P and F.

10. Programme: An educational programme leading to award of a degree, diploma or certificate.

11. Semester Grade Point Average (SGPA): It is a measure of performance of work done in a semester. It is ratio of total credit points secured by a student in various courses registered in a semester and the total course credits taken during that semester. It shall be expressed up to two decimal places.

12. Semester: Each semester will consist of 15-18 weeks of academic work equivalent to 90 actual teaching days. The odd semester may be scheduled from July to December and even semester from January to June.

13. Transcript or Grade Card or Certificate: Based on the grades earned, a grade certificate shall be issued to all the registered students after every semester. The grade certificate will display the course details (code, title, number of credits, grade secured) along with SGPA of that semester and CGPA earned till that semester.

B. Components or Constituents of Choice Based Credit System

There are five ingredients or components of the choice-based credit system that need to be cared and organized well in the successful working of the choice-based credit system. These are:

1. Adoption of the semester system
2. Making provision for the different types of courses and their teaching
3. Use of credit system
4. Use of Continuous and Comprehensive Evaluation (CCE)
5. Employment of Grading System

Let us discuss each of them one by one.

Adoption of the Semester System

Working with choice based credit system needs to change from the conventional annual system to semester system on the part of the colleges and universities. For this purpose an academic year needs to be divided into two semesters with a clear division and specification of the work done under these semesters (*e.g.* duration of teaching-learning engagements, and conduct of assessment or evaluation etc.). Here care is taken that the teaching work as well as assessment is performed semester-wise. However, a students' progress should be judged on the basis of the courses taken rather than time taken (like three years for science, arts, commerce or four years for engineering etc.). Each semester according to UGC norms needs to have a minimum of 90 teaching days for teaching-learning engagements.

Making provisions for the different types of course and their teaching

Choice based credit system is essentially characterized with having the provision of wide choices in terms of opting one or the other courses according to the needs and interests of the learners. In view of the guide lines issued by the UGC, courses in a programme (educational programme earning of degree) may be of three kinds outlined below.

1. Core Course: There may be a Core Course in every semester. This is the course which is to be compulsorily studied by a student as a core requirement to complete the requirement of a programme in a said discipline of study.

2. Elective Course: Elective course is a course which can be chosen from a pool of papers. It may be:

- Supportive to the discipline of study
- Providing an expanded scope
- Enabling an exposure to some other discipline/domain
- Nurturing student's proficiency/skill.

An elective may be "Generic Elective" focusing on those courses which add generic proficiency to the students. An elective may be "Discipline centric" or may be chosen from an unrelated discipline. It may be called an "Open Elective."

3. Foundation Course: The Foundation Courses may be of two kinds: Compulsory Foundation and Elective foundation. "Compulsory Foundation" courses are the courses based upon the content that leads to knowledge enhancement. They are mandatory for all disciplines. Elective Foundation courses are value-based and are aimed at man-making education.

In addition to these three types of courses, there may be also non-credit courses available in the institutions which will be assessed as 'Satisfactory' or 'Unsatisfactory'. These will not be included in the computation of SGPA/CGPA. However, all the three main courses will be accessed and evaluated to provide an effective and balanced result.

Use of Credit System

In the choice based credit system, each course (core, elective and foundation) is identified by a unique course code. All courses do not possess equal weightage. While designing syllabus, a course can have defined weightage. These weightage are called credits. When the student passes the course, he earns the credits which are based on that course. If a student passes a single course (subject or paper) in a semester, he does not have to repeat that course later. A student can earn credits according to his pace. If for some reasons, he cannot cope with the study load or if he falls sick, he has the freedom to study fewer courses and earn fewer credits and he can compensate this in the next semester.

How credits are computed?

In the prescribed courses for each semester, course credits are assigned on the basis of the number of hours required per week for lectures/tutorials/ lab work/field work to complete the course in a single semester. A study course may require direct teaching or lecturing (L) or tutorial (T), laboratory/ practical work or field work/project work (P). It can have only L components or only T or P components or combination of any two or all the three components. The basis of assigning credits for lecturing/tutoring as well as field work/project work/laboratory work is as under.

1 credit = 1 hour of direct teaching (lecturing or demonstrating) or tutoring per week

1 credit = 2 hours of laboratory work/field work/project work per week.

A course of 3 credits may be so designed as to have 2 credit for theory (lecturing/tutoring) and 1 credit for lab work/field work/project work.

A course of 4 credits may be so designed as to have 3 credits for theory (lecturing/tutoring) and 1 credit for lab work/field work/project work.

The credit frame work for the core, Elective and Foundation courses for a semester shall be as under

Core Compulsory	**Generic Elective**	**Compulsory Foundation**
Course I – 3 credits Course II-3 credits Total 6 credits per semester	2 credits per semester	2 credits per semester
Core Elective (Allied)	**Discipline centric elective/open elective**	**Elective Foundation**
Course I – 3 credits Course II – 3 credits Total 6 credits per semester	2 credits per semester	2 credits per semester

Core courses (compulsory and elective) thus shall have a total of 12 credits per Semester, Elective course (generic and elective) shall have 4 credits per semester and the Foundation courses (compulsory and elective) shall have 4 credits per semester. The normal graduation programme, thus, shall have 20 credits per semester and the total credits of all the six semester (under three academic years) shall be 120.

Besides a normal gradual programme a college/university may have the provision for honours and special level programmes (degree courses) and according a general frame work showing respective credits to be earned for passing out those programmes shall be as under.

Types of Programme	*Credit to be earned*
1. G (General Level Programme)	120 credits
2. A (Honours Level Programme)	140 credits
3. S (Special Level) 4 years BS programme	190 credits

Use of Continuous and Comprehensive Evaluation (CCE)

The implementation of choice based credit system needs to adopt the system of continuous and comprehensive evaluation for assessing or evaluating the learning outcomes of the students. A continuous assessment process in semester system is known popularly as internal assessment generally performed by the course teacher/instructor by a variety of means like written test, observation of the practical/laboratory work, seminars, field work, presentations, quizzes, group discussions and tutorials, etc. The feedback received through such continuous and formative evaluation should be used properly for bringing needed improvement in the ongoing teaching-learning process.

Employment of Grading System

Grading is a quite essential component of the choice based credit system. Grading can be performed by making use of the methods-relative grading or absolute grading as discussed earlier in this chapter.

The UGC recommends a 10-point grading system with the following letter grades as given below for the gradation of the students learning performance in each of the course of the semester.

Letter grade	*Grade point*
O (Outstanding)	10
A+ (Excellent)	9
A (Very Good)	8
B+ (Good)	7
B (Above Average)	6
C (Average)	5
P (Pass)	4
F (Fail)	0
Ab (Absent)	0

In addition to this, attempts will also be made to compute Semester Grade Point Average (SGPA) and Cumulative Grade Point Average (CGPA) for all the students. Let us see what are these and how are they computed.

Semester Grade Point Average (SGPA) indicates the overall performance of a student in a given semester. It is based on the total credit points earned by the student in all the courses and the total number of credits assigned to the courses in a semester. It is computed by the use of the following formula

$$\text{SGPA} = \frac{\text{Total credit points earned in a semester}}{\text{Total credits for that semester}}$$

Where credit point for a course included in the semester can be computed by using the formula given below:

Credit point for the course = No. of credits assigned for the course × Grade point secured in the course

Cumulative Grade Point Average (CGPA)

It shows overall performance of the student in all the courses of the all semesters of a programme helpful in earning the required degree. It is computed with the use of the following formula.

$$\text{CGPA} = \frac{\text{Total no. of credit points in all the semesters}}{\text{Total no. of credits in all the semester}}$$

An illustration of the Computation of SGPA and CGPA

(i) Computation of SGPA

Course	*Credit*	*Grade letter*	*Grade point*	*Credit Point* (*Credit* × *Grade*)
Course 1	3	A	8	3 × 8 = 24
Course 2	4	B+	7	4 × 7 = 28

Course 3	3	B	6	3 × 6 = 18
Course 4	3	O	10	3 × 10 = 30
Course 5	3	C	5	3 × 5 = 15
Course 6	4	B	6	4 × 6 = 24
	20			139

Thus, **SGPA =139/20 = 6.95**

(ii) Computation of CGPA

Sem. 1	*Sem. 2*	*Sem. 3*	*Sem. 4*	*Sem. 5*	*Sem. 6*
Credit: 20 SGPA: 6.9	Credit: 22 SGPA: 7.8	Credit: 25 SGPA: 5.6	Credit: 26 SGPA: 6.0	Credit: 26 SGPA: 6.3	Credit: 25 SGPA: 80

$$\text{Thus, CGPA} = \frac{20\times6.9+22\times7.8+25\times5.6+26\times6.0+26\times6.3+25\times8.0}{144}$$

$$= 6.73$$

Advantages of Choice Based Credit System (CBCS)

The overall advantages drawn by the adoption of choice based credit system may be summarized as below.

1. It allows to replace traditional teacher centered and subject centered approach with learner centered approach.
2. It has a great advantage in its offering wide choices and options for the study of a variety of subjects. The approach adopted for providing variety of choices is nick named as cafteria approach conveying the sense that one can have a thing of his choice to study and work in CBCS much in the same way as he gets things by placing order in the canteen.
3. It allows students to study with their own pace and to study one or the other course at his convenience.
4. It allows the students to study the courses beyond their own subject areas or disciplines. As a result a science student may have the opportunity to study the subjects belonging to humanity, commerce or language groups. It may enable them to gain knowledge and skills to other disciplines helpful in their all round growth and development.
5. It allows the students to opt for additional courses and achieve more than the required credits. Thus the creative, gifted and fast learners may get full opportunity for harnessing their energy in a fruitful way.
6. It has a big advantage in the name of transfer of credit helpful in
   - making the inter college/university migration possible for the needy students well with in the country and outside.
   - opting for one part of the course in one institute and the other part in another institute.

7. It allows the students for having more scope to enhance their skills and more scope of taking up projects and assignments, vocational training including entrepreneurship.
8. It can help in seeking needed cooperation and collaboration with the world of work, industries and employees for improving the skill potential of the country and providing job opportunities to the students.

Computer Based On-Line Examination

Computer based on-line examination represents a quite new emerging trend in the field of assessment or evaluation of the learning outcomes of the intended learners in the regular as well as on-line system of formal education.

Computer based on-line assessment or examination in its word meaning stands for a type of assessment or examination that is carried over on-line with the help of internet services or Local Area Network (LAN) of the computers. The main features as well as advantages of this computer-based online assessment or examination are summarized below

1. Here the test paper or assessment is delivered to the learner for assessing the desired learning outcomes on line through a computer connected to a network.

2. The contents of this test paper or assessment may differ depending upon the purposes served through assessment such as formative, diagnostic or summative.

3. In the field of education and especially in case of teaching-learning, On-line assessment is used primarily to measure cognitive abilities, demonstrating what has been learned after the occurrence of a particular educational event, such as the end of an instructional unit or chapter. When assessing practical abilities or to demonstrate learning that has occurred over a longer period of time an online portfolio (or ePortfolio) is often used. The first element that must be prepared when teaching an online course is assessment. Assessment is used to determine if learning is happening, to what extent and if changes need to be made.

4. The test paper appears on the screen of the computer before the examinee. He can now go through it for its responding. Usually there are multiple choice type questions included in the content of the test and the student/examinee is required to respond by clicking on one of the multiple choices.

5. On-line responding to the on-line test items carries a number of significant advantages to the students otherwise unavailable in the traditional paper-pencil tests. These have been properly emphasized in CBSE Website in connection with the employment of computer based on-line assessment in the manner as given below.

(i) The full contents of the test paper remain thoroughly open to the students at all times of their examination of assessment They can review or re-answer any question at any point of time during the examination.

(ii) The candidates enjoy the freedom of changing the option of the answer during the entire examination duration through a simple click of the mouse.

(iii) The candidates also has the option to mark any answer for review at later stage during the examination.

(iv) There lies a provision of showing all the question numbers in different colour scheme to indicate which of the questions have been answered, left unanswered and marked for review.

6. In addition to get assessed through the use of a test paper, students here may get opportunities for the desired assessment of their learning outcomes in many other useful forms like submission of assignments, project reports, field work and survey findings, etc.

7. The use of new technologies such as web, digital video, sound, animations, interactivity and audio-video conferencing facilities and mobile connectivity available on computer and smart phone devices have given an altogether exciting opportunities for the online assessment. It is now quite possible to assess the learning outcomes or performances of the students sitting far away from the teachers with the help of audio-video display and interaction available online over the computers, laptops and smart phones. One can assess the proceedings of a seminar, group discussion, group project, laboratory work, or the independent creative and constructive output of the students well while sitting on one's computer or working with smart phone quite conveniently in a most satisfactory way. He can provide essentially immediate feedback to his students and pass judgement over their efforts.

8. On-line assessment carried over computers/laptops/smart phones may prove quite helpful in carrying out various functions or purposes of evaluation in a quite satisfactory way such as

(i) using as a testing device for the assessment of previous knowledge before the teaching-learning of a concept.

(ii) fulfilling the needs and purposes of a diagnostic/formative/ summative test or evaluation.

(iii) providing a means and platform for practice testing as students have the option of getting them tested at their will as and when they require so.

Computer based online assessment thus can serve quite useful purposes in the assessment of learning as well as for learning in the field of regular and distance mode of teaching-learning. However, there lies a fear in its use expressed in general by the practitioners. It is related to academic dishonesty or cheating involved in the online assessment mostly in the form of identity fraud and plagiarism.

1. There are greater chances of identity fraud in online examination as one can appear for the other in answering the items online. To do away with such fraud the measures like below may be adopted.

- Use of supervised examination through the institutions testing center or require students to come in at a certain time for the examination.
- To get familiar with a student through their voice and appearance by communicating with the students through phone or audio-video conferencing.
- To personalize assignments to students backgrounds or current activities. This allows the student to apply it to their personal life and gives the instructor more assurance that the actual student is completing the assignment. Lastly, an instructor may not make the assignments heavily weighted so the students do not feel as pressured.

2. Plagiarism is the misrepresentation of another person's work. It is easy to copy and paste from the internet or retype directly from a source. It is not only the exact wordage, but the thought or idea. It is important to learn to properly cite a source when using someone else's work. Useful websites and software are also available for identifying this fraud.

Open Book Examinations

What is an Open Book Examination?

Open Book Examination represents one of the significant new approaches recommended for bringing reforms in the system of examination. *As a matter of definition an "open book examination" may be referred to an examination in which examinees are allowed to consult their class-notes, textbooks, and other approved material while answering questions.* It has been named as an open book examination only on account of the freedom to have a book open before the examinees while giving answers to the questions asked in their examination paper.

The rationale behind adopting Open Book Examination

What has made to opt for open book examinations is a pertinent question that can be raised for introducing this reformatory measure at any place and level of school or college education. The things like below may be mentioned in support of opting for open book examinations.

1. A cure for the menace of cheating and mass copying: It is not at all unusual during the examination to witness the scenes of cheating and copying on the part of examinees. It may also take a shape of mass copying at a particular examination center where students may be seen to be making use of copying material at a mass scale and their friends, senior students, professional and even parents helping them in their act of cheating and copying creating a lot of problems to the supervisory and school authorities.

The reason is very simple. The temptation is quite high. There seems to be an easy short cut for faring well in the examination by just copying the answer from the torn pages or photo copies of a text, help book or notes and all hue and cries in the examination centers lie in availing this illegal and immoral practice on the part of the majority of the examinees. A number of means and measures may be suggested to exercise checks and control over this evil and they have been under trial since a quite long time. However, earnestly speaking they have failed in their mission. There seems a ray of hope in switching over to open book examinations in place of the tradition system of closed book examinations. Let us take a bold step. Set the examinations questions in such a way as to leave no scope and use of copying and cheating and allow the examinees to use the class-notes, text books and other printing or photo material for answering these questions. The fuss in the name of cheating and copying in the examination will automatically stop.

2. Helpful in transforming learning process from information receiving to information processing: The other major rationale, lying behind the proposal of open book examination, is related with the nature of education we want to give to our future generation. In our schools classrooms we have been emphasizing on "dissemination of knowledge". The students are persuaded to receive the information or knowledge related to different subjects of the school curriculum though direct instruction or from the learning sources like text books and other help books available for this purpose. They are supposed to mug up this information and retain it in their memory for being used in answering the questions asked in their internal or external examinations. It is thus a memory level teaching-learning that has been practised in our schools for the teaching-learning and evaluation. At this age of rapid advancement, global competition and progress no country of the world can afford to plan and organizing the education of its citizens in such an indifferent way. The emphasis need to be shifted from receiving information to information processing at the hands of the children. They should be empowered to know and learn the way of acquiring knowledge rather than merely receiving it from their teachers and texts. We have to equip our children with the ability and skills of knowledge construction and information processing.

They should be helped in development of their cognitive abilities to build new knowledge and to apply available knowledge to solve problems and make intelligent decisions. The main focus of teaching-learning thus will be on the skills of acquiring, modifying and creating knowledge, that is, on processing information, rather than on the information content itself. It is therefore a need of the hour and necessity of the ongoing global changes that we have to switch over from an educational system based on transmission of knowledge and information to the construction and processing of the information. Needless to say, that our evaluation and examination system should also be modified and switched well in tune with the changes needed in the teaching-learning of our students.

We should stop asking such questions in the examinations that are totally dependent on the rote learning or memorization abilities of the students and that could be copied down or answered through the cheating and copying practices. Instead of it if we set such questions or get the examinees engaged in such activities that require the use of constructive, creative, logical, analytical, and other developed cognitive and applied skills or abilities of the students for testing their comprehension of the subject at the understanding and reflective level, then there hardly lies any risk in resorting to open book examination. It will help in removing the ill effects and melodrama of the rote learning and mechanical memorization. Students will not be having any phobia, anxiety and frustration of doing poorly on account of the failure of their memory at the time of responding to the questions. The facts and figures of the information required will be before them in the form of text books, class notes and other permissible printed material and they would be let free to provide proofs of their learning performances at the understanding and reflective levels instead of the memory level alone.

The reforms set in the mode of asking questions set in the examinations and system of open book examination introduced will automatically open the door of bringing appropriate modifications and improvement in the ongoing teaching-learning classroom practices. The emphasis will shift on the proper processing of information, construction of knowledge and development of creative and constructive faculties rather than mere transmission and reception of the information and knowledge and over dependence on direct instruction and mechanical memorization.

Types and Forms of Open Book Examinations

In terms of their forms and shapes, the open book examinations may be categorized as below

1. Unrestricted type of open book examinations: These are the type of open book examinations that truly depict the very nature and purpose of open book examinations. Here no unwanted restrictions are imposed on the examinees. They are free to take with them and consult any text book or help book (with or without scribbles on the margin), lecture handouts of the subject teacher, their own handwritten notes or any approved material or equipment for helping them in responding to the questions asked in the examination.

2. Restricted type of open book examinations: In the restricted type of open book examinations, students have no free access to texts, class notes and other printed material as happens in the case of unrestricted type of open book examinations. Here they may be permitted to consult printed documents such as the log tables, dictionaries, or prescribed texts of the subjects concerned, but no handwritten material or printed documents which have any scribbles on the margin or have no prior approval. Such unrestricted type of open book examinations neither represent the true concept of open book examinations nor have the required capability of fulfilling the missions and objectives of open book examinations.

The misconceptions and criticism about the practice of Open Book Examinations

The introduction of the scheme of open book examinations may be found to suffer from a number of misconceptions and criticism standing against its proper use and applications like below.

1. Disinterest and apathy of students towards learning: It is assumed as well as feared that the adoption of the practice of open book examination may make the students feel that there is no need of studying and preparing for the examinations as everything is available for them in the examination hall for responding to the examination questions. However, it is totally a misconception and misunderstanding about the practice of open book examinations. The situation is otherwise. It is true that students do not need to memorize and keep so many facts, formulae and information in their memory for their use at the time of providing answers to the examination questions as access to such information is readily available to them in the system of open book examination, yet a mere access to such information is not sufficient, they need to be able to apply it effectively. In Open Book examination one needs to quickly find the relevant information in the resources one has with him in the examination hall. It can only be possible when a learner is able to fully understand and be familiar with the content and materials of his subject. Moreover, the learners who give enough attention in studying and learning the course material at the understanding and reflective level can only respond well to the type of questions asked in the open book examinations. In this way the responsibilities of the learners are bit increased in the open book examinations rather than providing them scope for being negligent towards their learning and studying of the subject in a proper way.

2. Breeding negligence on the part of teachers: It is feared that the practice of open book examination may drift the teachers away from their teaching responsibilities by getting them feel that there is no use of teaching and making the students serious about their studies as they will have open access to the needed sources for answering questions in the examination hall. However, this assumption on the part of teachers that they need not to bother about the study of their students is quite improper. The facts stand quite contrary to this misbelief. A teacher in the system of open book examination has to be more alert, attentive and prepared for the study and development of their students as he has to guide and assist them for the thorough knowledge, understanding and application of the course material. He has to help them for their understanding and reflective level of learning, develop their potential for the proper processing of the acquired information and make them capable of using their cognitive abilities for responding to the questions needing problem solving ability and creative or constructive imagination.

3. Making mockery of the examination or evaluation: It is also feared as well alleged that the adoption of open book examination will result in making mockery of the actual process of assessing and evaluating the students' performance or the process and products of teaching-learning outcomes. However, such fear and allegation does not hold much ground. In fact it is a better approach for testing and evaluating the real worth of the students in terms of their learning at the needed understanding and reflective levels. It is true that it does not provide undue importance and advantage to the learners' rote learning and memorization ability and do not test the level of retaining information but it tries to test their other essential abilities, skills and potential helpful in the proper understanding and application of the course contents. Therefore it is quite worthwhile to make use of the open books examination practice and the fears and allegation against its use are ill founded.

The impact and implications of the practice of Open Book Examinations

The adoption of open book examinations will exercise a sizable impact over the whole system and process of education mainly mentioned as below.

A. Impact over teachers and their teaching

1. Teachers will have to work more in preparing students for facing the challenges put up by the introduction of open book examination practice. Since the questions asked in these examinations will need the use of appropriate mental skills, creativity and constructivism on the part of students. Teachers will have to work for the development of such skills and abilities among their students.

2. The teachers' role will be changed from a mere information giver to a facilitator, guide, trainer, consultant and assessor. Accordingly, they will now switch over their teaching functions from prescriptive to the provocative, from providing knowledge to empowering students to acquire knowledge, from furnishing students with a finite body of knowledge to equipping them with higher order cognitive skills and from dependency to taking ownership of the learning experience.

3. There will be a complete paradigm shift in the use of teaching methods, strategies and techniques on the part of teachers. Methods involving direct instruction, mechanical memorization and habit formation will not work. The behaviouristic approach of teaching will have to be replaced by cognitive and constructive approaches or methods of teaching. As a result, attempts will be made to shift the focus from teaching a body of information to teaching how to process and apply it.

4. Consequently the strategies like guided discovery, problem solving method, collaborative and cooperative learning, project and activity centered approach and self- study and assignment based teaching-learning programmes will be promoted and efforts will be made to provide opportunities for the students do make use of their mental abilities for solving challenging problems, analyzing and synthesizing the given facts and reason out new ways and methods of doing things.

5. Here as far as the overall nature of the teachers' teaching is concerned, the main focus of teaching will shift on the skills of acquiring, modifying and creating knowledge, that is, on processing information, rather than on the information content itself. In other words, teaching will no longer be the transfer of information from the teacher to students. It will be the training of the mind in certain intellectual skills.

B. Impact over students and their learning

1. The most immediate impact on students will be that they will stop "mugging" or rote learning. The focus of learning will shift from a memory level learning to understanding and reflective levels of learning.

2. It will put a halt to their habit of copying and cheating in the examinations.

3. The challenges put up by the type of questions asked in the examinations and the techniques and preparation needed for taking advantages of books and printing material available in examination hall may demand from the students to engage in active and meaningful learning. They will now try to learn the way of acquiring information, constructing knowledge with their own attempts and processing the acquired information for solving the faced problem and answering the raised issue.

C. Impact over the framing of the test questions

The significant changes will be now visible in the nature of the test questions framed for the open book examinations. There will be no use of asking the questions like "When the first battle of Panipat was held and who were involved in this battle?" "Tell about the phenomenon of solar eclipse or lunar eclipse." Students can easily find their answers in the books and material available to them in the examination hall, and copy them in their answer books. The test framers have to take care of the fact that the aim is not to test the rote learning and information retaining ability of the students. They have to design such test questions and programme the administration of the test in such a way as to make it capable of: (i) testing the students' understanding of the acquired knowledge of a course, and the skills of applying that understanding in a maximum useful way, (ii) discouraging the tendency of copying the answers of the questions from the books and notes.

Knowing so far, thus we may now conclude that open book examination system can be really credited as a quite bold and big step for bringing needed reforms in the prevalent system of examinations. Tried in a proper way it can surely help in restoring the true meaning of the word education for both teachers and students. There may be some difficulty in setting the right type of questions in the beginning, but it will go away soon if genuine attempts will be made by the researchers and teachers for doing so.

Question Banks

As the name suggests, these are the banks or treasures (available in the printed and bound form or computer software) from where we can have a number of questions set on each subject for the evaluation of the students. Emphasizing upon the need of maintaining such treasury of questions, National Curriculum Framework (NCF), 2005 has put up its views in the following words.

> "*In order to improve the validity of current examinations, the entire process of paper setting needs to be overhauled. The focus should shift to framing good questions rather than more paper setting. Such questions need not to be generated by experts only. Through wide canvassing, good questions can be pooled all year around, from teachers, college professors in that discipline, educators from other states, and even students. These questions, after careful vetting by experts, could be categorized according to level of difficulty, topic/area, concept/competency being evaluated and time estimated to solve. These could be maintained along with a record of their usage and testing record to be drawn upon at the time of generating question papers.*" (NCF 2005: 114)

Viewing in this manner the use of question bank may prove quite advantageous and helping hand to the paper setters in terms of the supply of well framed and standardized set of questions for various class levels and learning areas.

However, besides serving the need of supplying questions of good quality to the teachers and paper setters for the one or the other examinations, these may also be found to serve the following useful purpose of a good evaluation in the areas and aspects like below:

- In the diagnostic task carried out by the teachers for their students.
- To the teacher at the introductory, developing and final stage of his lesson.
- Drill work and home assignment can be properly given with the help of these questions.
- Need of the individual differences can be successfully met with the variety of questions available with varying difficulty levels.
- In the development of the instructional programme, curriculum, and instructional strategies, these questions can be very well utilized.
- To have questions well related to the instructional objectives of all the behavioural domains and levels.
- In the proper scoring and interpretation of the student responses.
- In providing proper instructions to the examiners and examinees.
- In organizing teaching and learning at all the three levels – memory, understanding and reflective.
- To set before the learners the required learning objectives and keep them purposefully motivated in the classroom instructional work or self-study.

Regarding their overall impact and usefulness it can be well said that the questions available from questions banks are framed with utmost care with all the technical formalities and statistical soundness, so that these may help in proper evaluation of the potential and learning outcomes of the students.

As regards the availability of these question banks, we may approach NCERT and SCERT's located in various states, UGC, Universities, colleges, state libraries, various examining and testing bodies and private publishers etc.

On Demand Examination in Distance Education Mode of IGNOU

The scheme of on-demand examination is fully operational in the distance education system governed by IGNOU, New Delhi. It is being implemented for more than 135 courses run in distance education mode with the help of 18 regional centres. It provides opportunity to the students for appearing in on-Demand Exam as per their need and convenience. The software for generating individualized question papers and for on-line registration for on-Demand exam have been developed in-house in NCIDE with the help the Students Evaluation Division, Regional Services Division and the Regional Centres of IGNOU, the scheme of On-Demand Examination is now fully operational. The unique features of scheme include online submission of registration fee, issue of online hall ticket, online attendance record, etc. The software can generate a large number of unique and parallel question papers exactly in accordance with the design and blueprint provided by the faculty.

Presently the facility of on-Demand Examination is available in 135 courses of different programmes through 18 Regional Centres of IGNOU, including Aizwal, Bhubneswer, Cochin, Chennai, Dehradun, Delhi-1, Delhi-2, Hyderabad, Jabalpur, Jammu, Jaipur, Karnal, Koraput, Madurai, Nagpur, Noida, Ranchi and Srinagar.

The Main Advantages Drawn through the System On-Demand Examination (ODE)

The main advantages available through a system of on-Demand examination may be briefed as below.

- It allows the student to take examination when he/she is ready. Readiness depends on the Student and not on the institution.
- It permits the student to choose the date of his/her examination.
- It reduces the threat of failure in examination.
- It removes frustration, loss of self esteem, peer group ridicule, and depression that are generally characterized by the Term-End Examination.
- Under ODE, the degree and level of performance is decided by the student who can reappear in the examination as many times as he/she wants, till satisfied.
- ODE is also helpful in containing malpractices in examinations, as it is a system where the tools for evaluation are unique for individual student. The question paper for each student is different having comparable difficulty level.
- ODE respects the *individuality* and *sovereignty* of the student.

References and Suggested Readings

Adams, G.R. and Schvaneveldt, J.D., *Understanding Research Methods*, (2nd ed.), New York: Longman, 1991.

Adams, G.S. Measurement and Evaluation in Education, Psychology and Guidance, New York: Holt, Rinehart and Winston, 1964.

Ahmans, J.S. and Glock, M., *Evaluating Pupil Growth,* Boston: Allyn and Bacon, 1959.

Best, J.W. and Kahn, J.V., *Research in Education*, (10th edition), New Delhi: PHI Learning Pvt. Ltd., 2010.

Bhargava, Mahesh, *Modern Psychological Testing and Measurement*, (VII ed.), Agra: Harprasad Bhargava, 1987.

Bloom, B.S., Hasting, J.T. and Madaus, G.F., *Hand Book on Formative and Summative Evaluation of Student Learning*, New York: McGraw-Hill, 1971.

Bloomers, P and Lindquist, B.F., *Elementary Statistical Methods in Psychology and Education*, New York: Houghton Mifflin, 1960,

Crisewell in J.L. Moreno, *The Sociometric Reader*, Glencoe, Illinois: *The Free Press*, 1960.

Cronbach, L.J., *Essentials of Psychological Testing* (3rd ed.), New York: Harper and Row, 1970.

Encyclopaedia Britannica, Erickson, F. (1985), Qualitative Methods in Research on Teaching in M.C. Wittrock (Ed.), *Hand Book of Research on Teaching* (3rd edition), New York: Macmillan, pp. 119-161

Garrett, H.E., *Statistics in Psychology and Education* (6th Indian ed.), Vakils, Feffer and Simon, Bombay: 1971.

Good, C.V., *Dictionary of Education*, New York: McGraw-Hill, 1959.

Gronlund, N.E. and R.L. Linn, *Measurement and Evaluation in Teaching*, (5th ed.), New York: Macmillan,1990.

Loftland, J. *Analysing Social Settings: A Guide to Qualitative Observation and Analysis*, Belmont, CA: Wedsworth.

Moreno, Jacob Levy, *Who shall survive?* Beacon, NY: Beacon House 1934, Revised edition 1953

NCERT, *National Curriculum Frame Work for School Education*, New Delhi: NCERT Publication Department, 2005.

Report of the Secondary Education Commission (1952-53), New Delhi: Ministry of Education, Govt. of India, 1953.

Report of Education Commission (1964-66), New Delhi: Ministry of Education, Govt. of India (1966).

Remmers, H.H., Gage, N.L. and Rumel, J.F., *A Practical Introduction to Measurement and Evaluation*, New York: Harper and Row, 1960.

Stufflebeam, D.L. *et al.*, *Educational Evaluation and Decision Making*, Bloomington: Phi Delta, Kappa, 1971.

Tate, M.W., *Statistics in Education*, New York: McGraw-Hill, 1956.

Torgerson, T.L. and Adams, G.S., *Measurement and Evaluation*, New York: John Wiley, 1966.

Wrightstone, J.W., Hustman, J. and Robbins, G., Evaluation in Modern Education, New York: American Book Company, 1956.